In the Eye o

CW00520956

In the Eye of
Past the Zonnules of Zinn,
Is a land ringed by Wyrms
And the Dragons of Odin.

or

A History of Cumbria

or

The Saga of Yan and Tan

H. G. Wills

ARTHUR H. STOCKWELL LTD
Torrs Park, Ilfracombe, Devon, EX34 8BA
Established 1898
www.ahstockwell.co.uk

By the same author:
The Best Kept Secrets of the Western Marches
Room 22 Revisited

ISBN 978-0-7223-4810-9
Printed in Great Britain by
Arthur H. Stockwell Ltd
Torrs Park   Ilfracombe
Devon EX34 8BA

IN THE EYE OF STORMS

Yan and Tan, two brothers and members of the species *Ovo bipedus*, are encouraged by their father, Professor Tethra Hardwick of Wiggonby College, to discover the real history of Cumbria. They embark on what will turn out to be a *saga* and are helped by a group of fellow Cumbrians, including Dubston Skree, Jean d'Allelle, Carvetius Brock, Chibb Swaledale, Bangalore Locksley and Colonel Windermere Robinson. From time to time, a mysterious figure, whose name and appearance alters with the passage of time and circumstances, mentors the Hardwick boys, but he is not all he seems to be.

Lurching from one adventure to another, the intrepid heroes avoid hitmen from Archaeologists Anonymous and steadfastly refuse to accept the insidious censorship of the Historical Hogwash Society. Their vigilance and powers of enquiry open doors into the past, previously hidden from prying eyes.

The Hardwick brothers' tale begins with the early post-glacial migrations and explores the onset of Celtic civilisation in North-Western Europe. They reveal how the Roman colonisation of Cumbria eventually gave way to a second resurgence of Celtic culture and the appearance of kingdoms, like Rheged. With skill they tease out the complex story of five of the eight Scandinavian invasions, which enveloped the country in a 600-year period of turmoil, from which England would emerge along with a reunited Cumbria.

Their journey all but completed, Yan and Tan Hardwick make even greater discoveries, which their father had suspected – ones which would alter their lives for ever.

Essentially, this is history without the boring bits. The pure historical facts are there for all to read – along with an analysis of both a genetic study of the migration of ethnic groups and the impact of their languages on modern place names. To lighten the whole tale, there is also a liberal injection of humour, legend, whimsy, satire and surrealism, which impact on the very basis of evolution itself – to say nothing of revealing the unseen forces swirling in and around a county known only to as few as Midgard.

H. G. Wills, 15 May 2017.

CONTENTS

A List of Illustrations and Maps   7

Acknowledgements and Clarifications   9

Editor's Note   11

Introduction   13

A List of Chapters:

   1.   Tulley Mowze's Library   17

   2.   Blokey Bill's Flying Circus   21

   3.   A Trail of Stone Breadcrumbs and Ice   25

   4.   Genetics and 'Stuff'   33

   5.   A Cat amongst the Pigeons   43

   6.   Mare of the Celts   47

   7.   Sinister Dexter – Dog of War   57

   8.   The Really Dim Ages   69

   9.   Angrboda's Sandwich   81

  10. A Cold Wind from across the North Sea   85

  11. Life in the Faslane with Ivar the Boneless and Olaf the White 93

  12. Pothole No. 6,459,778 at Myth's End   105

  13. Norse, South, East and West   117

  14. A Great Dane in Gosforth and a Game of Norse and Crosses   129

Appendices (Maps and Explanatory Lists):

   1.   Cumbria   138

   2.   The Romans in Cumbria   140

   3.   Hadrian's Wall   144

   4.   The Anglo-Saxon Kingdoms of Britain   148

   5.   Northumbrian/Anglian Cumbria   152

   6.   Norse Cumbria   155

Bibliography   161

A LIST OF ILLUSTRATIONS AND MAPS

Front Cover – In the Eye of Storms

1.	A Cup of Ellis Tea	10
2.	Yan and Tan in Their Political Days	12
3.	Cumbria	16
4.	T'uther Tower	20
5.	The Road to Dubb's Hut	24
6.	The Ice Age – 20,000 BC	29
7.	The Late Glacial Period – 13,000 BC	30
8.	Genetics	32
9.	Doggerland – 16,000 BC	38
10.	The Northern European Coastline – 7000 BC	39
11.	The Vera/Velda Haplogroup Migration – 14,000 BC	40
12.	The Ruy Haplogroup Migration – 10,000 – 5000 BC	41
13.	The Cat with six Legs	42
14.	Deep Thought at Lowca	46
15.	The Celtic Tribes of Northern Britannia	54
16.	Brythonic/Cumbric Cumbria	55
17.	Sinister Dexter – Dog of War	56
18.	Roman Cumbria	64
19.	Hadrian's Wall	65
20.	The Origins of Auxiliary Troops in Northern Britannia	66
21.	Faraday – The Electric Dog	68
21.	The Provinces of Britannia in AD 193	74
22.	The Provinces of Britannia in AD 293	75
23.	The Kingdom of the North – circa AD 410–450	76
24.	Northern Britain – circa AD 450	77
25.	Northern Britain – circa AD 600	78
26.	Blokey's Latest Disguise	80
27.	The Laeti	84
28.	Anglo-Saxon Britain – circa AD 700	89
29.	Northumbrian/Anglian Cumbria	90
30.	The Lost Word of Ragnar 'Hairy Breeches' Lothbrok	92

31. Danish Raids – AD 798–865   98
32. Danish Settlements – AD 835–1035   99
33. The Great Heathen Army – AD 865–866   100
34. The Great Heathen Army – AD 866–869   101
35. The Great Heathen Army – AD 870–871 – Ivar the Boneless   102
36. The Great Heathen Army – AD 875 – Halfdan Ragnarsson   103
37. The Pie-King of Iceland   104
38. The Lands Under Danelaw – AD 878   111
39. The Dismemberment of Danelaw – AD 911–927   112
40. Olaf Guthfrithson – AD 929   113
41. The Campaigns of King Edmund I of England – AD 942–944   114
42. Speatrie, near Bifrost Bridge and Valhalla   116
43. Norse Raids – AD 750–864   123
44. Norse Settlements – AD 800–1014   124
45. Norse Cumbria – Map 1   125
46. Norse Cumbria – Map 2   125
47. St Columba and St Martin's Cross on Iona   128
48. Aethelred the Unready's Payments of Danegeld – AD 980–1005   131
49. Knud – The Great Dane   132
50. Gosforth Cross   135

Back Cover – Yan and Tan – Unsung Heroes

ACKNOWLEDGEMENTS AND CLARIFICATIONS

I should like to acknowledge the assistance afforded me by Professor Stephen Oppenheimer and his permission to use the maps concerning the migration routes of the Vera/Velda, R1b-13 and R1b-10 haplogroups, in Chapter 4, which I have adapted from those in his book *The Origins of the British*, published by Robinson of London (2006) – a book which I would heartily recommend.

With regard to the other books, maps and DVDs which formed the basis of my research into the history of Cumbria, there is an extensive bibliography following the appendices.

During the telling of the saga of Yan and Tan Hardwick, numerous characters are encountered and a number of organisations are referred to. Needless to say, all are fictitious and have no basis in reality. Any similarity to persons, either living or deceased, or to associations, whether extinct or extant, is entirely coincidental.

H. G. Wills.

A Cup of Ellis Tea

"Words are worth a lot to me,"
The poet said one day at tea
Next to a southern lake,
Whilst eating his favourite chocolate cake.

His dear sister, 'Kindly-Dot',
Picked up a blue ceramic pot
And gave her Bill another brew.
"I bought it, m'dear – just for you.

"It's special stuff or so I'm told
And worth its weight in Aztec gold.
Comes from near Khartoum –
A tincture of a red mushroom."

"I know exactly what you mean –
I see it all in Velvatine,
Just by the purple macaroons
Past the trees of silver spoons.

"Far beyond the turquoise screes
Above the mountains made of cheese.
They fly like drunken terrapins
That golden host of Zeppelins."

EDITOR'S NOTE

Beatrix Potter, truly a light in a dark and dreary world, would have us believe that Cumbria is the home of talking rabbits, hedgehogs, ducks, frogs and the like. This is a charming thought, but not entirely true, and is the sort of thing we might tell our children. However, what is not commonly known is that *Homo sapiens* is not the only sentient bipedal mammalian life form in the county – there are in fact two others.

Neanderthals can still be found, despite the fable of their extinction during the last Ice Age. Heavily disguised, such unhappy creatures have found gainful employment in politics, social work and football.

The third member of this trio is *Ovo bipedus*, which, to the unsympathetic eye, has an appearance similar in some respects to that of sheep, which is not entirely coincidental as it was from that species – many millions of years ago – that they evolved.

How they actually came to be in Cumbria is, as the historians are fond of saying, not entirely clear. Some believe that around 14,000 BC they accompanied a human hunter-gatherer haplogroup, called 'Ruisko', from South-Western Europe to Scandinavia. Whether they subsequently travelled to the Cumbria area from Norway in the late Neolithic period, the Bronze Age or even much later – with the Norse settlers around AD 900 – is open to archaeological conjecture or to a semi-scientific academic manoeuvre, commonly referred to as 'spin of a bottle'. Certainly, there is a strong belief that Herdwick sheep came over with the Vikings and may, perhaps, have been accompanied by a few members of *Ovo bipedus*.

This group is, as it happens, a very intelligent, artistic and thoughtful species, as a poem by Professor Tethra Hardwick of Wiggonby College – 'A Cup of Ellis Tea' – readily demonstrates. It should also be noted that a very laudable characteristic of this group, which *Homo sapiens* lacks, is, that it does not look down on its living distant ancestors. Professor Hardwick also believes that evolution may not entirely be a one-way street and, to reinforce this argument, is fond of saying at dinner parties that he has frequently seen humans eating bananas in both Workington and Carlisle.

Having set the record straight, it is now time to tell the saga of Yan and Tan Hardwick, and their unbiased history of Cumbria or, as some have been tempted to call it, Midgard.

It all began not too many years ago. . . .

Yan and Tan Hardwick in their political days, when they stood in a parliamentary by-election in Carlisle sometime in the mid 1960s as joint candidates for the People's Party of Free Cumbria.

INTRODUCTION

In a disused but fairly habitable Cold War bunker not far from the abandoned Blue Streak Testing Silos just north of the A69 in Gilsland, a collection of academics had been unwillingly corralled together – each group strenuously ignoring the others.

On the left was a 'scroll' of historians – some were blinkered; others sucked their thumbs; a few listened to talking books and one proudly held aloft a placard on which was written in joined-up writing a profound thought for all the whole world to see: 'Historians are neither fanciful nor dickslegzic.'

Next to them stood a 'dig' of archaeologists, who looked friendly enough but were gathered round an object which one of them had recently dug up. It was a broken glass receptacle found on the doorstep of a Neolithic round house on which four embossed letters – M, I, L and K – were clearly visible.

"We found a number of these on the doorsteps of six roundhouses . . . but what they mean is a mystery," their team leader declared to his colleagues, who all nodded and scratched their heads in bewilderment.

In the centre of the room a 'cacophony' of four linguists, each attired in national costume, were standing nose to nose and cursing each other – but to no avail, as each one was totally unaware of the language the others were bellowing in.

At the back of the room in a gloomy corner was a 'quarry' of palaeontologists and geologists, who were rather noisily chewing on an assortment of mixed chocolate-coated ammonite shells and caramelised trilobite tails taken by the handful from a large hessian sack labelled 'Toothy Belgian Delights'.

Finally, sitting all alone, knitting a double helix in llama wool, was the thoughtful Dr Jean d'Allelle, a geneticist, who could have contributed much to the proceedings had he been able to get a word in edgeways. Missing a stitch, he looked up in frustration and, out the corner of his eye, espied two well-dressed but clearly ovine-looking bipeds, striding up to a pool of light in the centre of the stage, where a mahogany lectern stood.

With a single blast from his pocket Klaxon, Mr Tan, who often used the device on telephone cold-callers, caught the attention of the 'academics'. Then his brother, Mr Yan, spoke in a Cumbrian accent, but with undoubted authority.

"We have been sent here by owa fatha, Professor Tethra Hardwick, the Dean of Wiggonby College in the Grand Duchy of Gamelsby, which, as you all know, is twinned both with the Sorbonne in Paris, whose motto is '*Un chien peut regarder une évêque*', and with La Sapienza di Roma, with its unforgettable warning of '*Ira dyspepsiam facit.*'

"It's all painfully simple," continued Yan. "You – you *Sapiens* – have collectively made such a cat's backside of the history of Cumbria that the public has not the slightest inkling about the truth concerning our county's past. So," he continued, "short of resorting to mental torture – forcing you to watch men waving their arms and legs about whilst kicking a football in the vain attempt to make their brains work – you are required to correct the error of your ways and work together to produce a simple but readable account of Cumbria's past, which the college will then publish."

It would be a pleasant surprise to announce that the proposed venture, as outlined above, came to pass. Sadly it did not, as shortly after Yan Hardwick had ended his exhortation a gradual murmuring noise arose from the 'academics', who had reverted to small-group discussions and self-indulgent gratification. Thus, in almost unbearable despair and shrouded in the blanket of failure, Yan and Tan left the bunker. Outside, next to a van selling deep-fried battered Scottish Mars Bars, was a souped-up Austin 7, into which they climbed. Their journey back to Wiggonby was not a happy one.

"We were not successful, Fatha," intoned the brothers in unison.

"Hardly surprising" was the reply. "Truth to tell, *Homo sapiens* and *Ovo bipedus* have never got on that well. We both left Africa together – around 120,000 years ago – but they preferred the company of their Neanderthal mates and headed south to the Mediterranean on a jolly-boys spree. We, I believe, headed north . . . but then, as the 'historians' are fond of saying, nobody really knows.

"Well, I guess it's now up to you lads to write a history of Cumbria. All the information you require is at hand in the library of Tulley Mowze, your great-great-granfatha. Go to it, afore the *Sapiens* beat you to the punch and print off another load of 'History Kett'.

And so it was that the Brothers Hardwick began their life's work, which to this day is, inexplicably, still not read by many of their distant cousins on the Caldbeck Fells . . . but it is quite popular in Speatrie, only a little distance to the north-west.

CUMBRIA

CHAPTER 1 – TULLEY MOWZE'S LIBRARY

The library was situated below their father's study and the shortest route to it was through an oak-panelled door across the hall and down a stone-faced spiral staircase. After descending two flights, Yan and Tan finally emerged into an enormous cavern-like low-ceilinged room, which seemed to go on forever – disappearing into a distant gloom on either side of them. There were books upon books, as far as the eye could see, not just on shelves, but stacked against the stone walls. The air had a musty odour and the chill of February.

Immediately in front of them, on a refectory table supported by solid and demonically clawed legs, were two uneven stacks of large atlases, between which could be seen a small, but otherwise unremarkable, seated man.

This, they both surmised, was Frank 'Fuss' Potts, a former chartered accountant who had found his former employment far too exciting and leapt headlong into the unfathomed emotional void of Wiggonby College's reference library, where he had risen to the post of head librarian. Apart from being an avid stamp and matchbox collector, Frank Potts had a profound interest in toponymy, which the map on the wall behind him did not, in any way, reveal.

"Yes, I know what you're thinking" were his first words. "The map has no names on it whatsoever. It has any number of villages, towns, rivers, lakes, valleys and mountains on it, but I haven't had time to add the names yet . . . . The study of how places got their names and when . . . is very difficult and time-consuming . . . and – Mr Potts stopped quite abruptly and very short of breath. "Sorry . . . forgot to breathe. . . . I get so engrossed talking about my hobbies!"

"Life truly is a bitch, Mr Potts," murmured Tan without any great conviction or sympathy.

"We're here to do some research – the Dean sent us," intoned Yan.

"Yes, I know . . . he telephoned."

"Well, where do we start?" they both groaned in unison, looking at the thousands of books around them.

"The beginning's always a good place," suggested Mr Potts.

"The beginning?"

"Yes! Come back tomorrow. Reading material for each of you will be set out in Alcove No. 1 . . . and, if you're interested in toponomy, I could . . . "

Frank's voice tailed off as the boys turned and left with undue speed.

Alcove No.1 contained two chairs and two desks, suspended above which was a sign written in the finest of copperplate writing, which simply said, 'The Beginning'.

Before either of the boys could say a word, a figure emerged from nowhere and bleated in a particularly high-pitched voice, "My name is Chibb Swaledale. I am the assistant librarian . . . as was my father, Blogg, before me . . . and any references to a Chibb off the Old Blogg would not be appreciated. Now, Mr Potts, as it happens, is far too busy with his map and has asked me to look after you."

"Much appreciated, Mr Swaledale."

"And, if you're peckish, there are some light refreshments in Alcove No. 2 – some rhubarb-and-dock cordial and a plate of sphagnum bhajis which my dear wife, Melancholia, made with her fair hands yesterday."

Then, without much ado, Chibb Swaledale turned on his heels and disappeared as silently as he had arrived.

"And what do you make of Chibb, then?" enquired Tan.

"Not sure," came the reply, "but I think he's been round the Wigton Pump . . . at least twice!"

Truth to tell, he had completed three circuits.

The best of the books which Chibb had left on the table were as follows:

1) *Turned Out Nice Again, but a Bit Cold* by Professori Giorgio Formbini.

2) *The Origin of the Peaches* by Fitzroy and Snuffly the Beagle.

After an hour Tan abandoned the unequal struggle and strolled over to Alcove No. 2, finally reappearing thirty minutes later, brushing some crumbs off his tweed jacket.

"Well, Yan, what have you learned? My book was all about a cruise to Isla Isabela and a search for lizards and tortoises – riveting stuff, but no real help to us."

"Actually, Signor Formbini's book could be of help. It's all about the Ice Age."

Tan was not impressed, but nevertheless picked up another tome of easy reading: *A Swashbuckling Tale of Neolithic Archaeology* by Montgomery Dullpencil. Yan was even luckier. He found *Life on the Edge: A Discourse on Toponomy* by Frank Potts.

After three to four weeks the boys were beginning to flag, and after five both sought solace in watching an old recording of a Christmas football derby between Carlisle United and Workington Reds – circa 1963. The highlight of the match was the half-time parade of Olga the Stuffed Fox around the cinder track overlooking the steelworks. During the game, Workington's player-manager was cheered incessantly by the opposing Blues and given encouragement in the form of friendly taunts, such as "Dirty Furfey" and "The ref's a ****** and so are you!"

Continuing the suspension in their endeavours, the boys headed to the Legless Sailor.

"If I read another account of one more digger unearthing a broken pot or examining a soil stain, I swear I shall . . ." intoned Yan, who was at the end of his tether.

"And what's with all these tiny numbers all over the pages? Are they so forgetful that they have to litter their histories with afterthoughts?" his brother complained.

"They write and write about what they've unearthed," said Yan, "but they never join up the dots or make any sense of anything. Perhaps one day, when they've dug up the whole of the country, they'll leave and volunteer to count all the grains of sand in the Sahara!"

"No doubt, but listen to this," replied Tan. "Last week I read 300 pages of really turgid stuff compiled by a 'clot' of historians, archaeologists and linguists, who finally after months of heated debate proclaimed to the world that the Celts spoke Celtic! I could have written that on the back of a fag packet!"

On the walk back home, Tan turned to Yan and said, "I wish – I do wish we had just a little help from somewhere or someone."

Now, we must all be very careful about what we wish for, as there are forces at work around us about which we know nothing. And sometimes they eavesdrop on our conversations and even grant our dearest wishes.

T'uther Tower

"Eee, by gum
And shake your bum,
We must 'ave one o' those!"
Mayor Bickerstaffe blurted out
Almost in a shrieking shout.
He gazed up and caught an eyeful
Of the wondrous tower
Built by that Gustave Eiffel.
Passers-by thought him quite insane
And threw him head first into the River Seine.

But thanks t'Mayor's brilliant foresight
Blackpool now boasts a cracking delight.
The people cry out with jubilations,
Especially durin' t'illuminations.
When its thousand bulbs emit a light
Which shines so brightly every night.
We're prouder of it than the red rose –
Much more indeed than you might suppose,
For one is just a bloody flower
But t'uther's the fantastic Blackpool Tower.

CHAPTER 2 – BLOKEY BILL'S FLYING CIRCUS

The next morning both boys were suffering from a mixture of dehydration, nausea, headache and lack of enthusiasm for the task in hand. Noise was also a problem, which a cheerful and boisterous Chibb could not control.

He blurted out, "You have a large postcard from Blackpool . . . with a poem and an invitation!"

"Some cordial, please . . . Melancholia's special poppy juice" was all Tan managed to say.

Yan picked up the mail. "It's from someone called Bill Blokey or Blokey Bill, and he's sending an aeroplane to pick us up at Carlisle's international airport."

Enquiries about their host were met with blank stares, but their father did ask rather ominously, "What have you done?"

And, like most children, all the boys could muster was "Nothing!"

A twin-engined Dakota, painted in garish colours, sat on the runway at Houghton and, lest there be any doubt as to the owner of the aircraft, the words 'Blokey Bill's Flying Circus' in letters three feet high had been painted on both wings as well as on the fuselage.

The uniformed and well-groomed female cabin crew ushered their guests into a tastefully decorated interior. Ovine-friendly drinks were served and within minutes the plane was airborne. Flying at 11,000 feet in a cloudless sky, Yan and Tan gazed out of the windows and took in the full magnificence of the county below them.

Yan was, as ever, the first to speak. "I know it sounds absolutely stupid, but Cumbria really does look exactly like a map!"

The air hostess who had just served them the hair of a very big dog smiled and could not resist retelling her favourite anecdote for the hundredth time. "Once, when working for a holiday company, I overheard a woman say with surprise as we passed through a solid carpet of rainclouds above

Manchester, 'Eeeeh, the sun's shining up here!' – which was a great relief to everyone, as the galaxy was not supposed to end for at least another six months."

It wasn't long before they were descending, and then in the last fifty feet or so Tan also made an observation which rang true: "With the tower on the flat, wide horizon, it reminds me a little of the old steam-train journeys across the Solway Plain with the spire of Silloth's church in the distance."

"Quite so," Yan recalled, as they touched down.

The transport to the tower was an open-topped converted 1907 Rolls-Royce Silver Ghost – a thing once of beauty was now just a circus clown's car. The private elevator up to the penthouse suite was located in the menagerie – actually in a cage labelled 'Ferocious Hungry Velociraptors', which was fortunately empty.

"Keeps the Wakes Week crowds out – well, some of them anyway!" the 'minder' confided through gritted teeth with a less than sincere smile. "Mr Blokey is through the middle door – don't go through either of the other two unless you want a very quick exit to the Golden Mile!"

Foreboding was exactly what the boys were experiencing at that precise moment – but, as luck would have it, it turned out nice again and their misapprehension soon evaporated.

"Good day. And you must be Tan . . . and you Yan," said a jovial figure in a maroon smoking jacket – which was quite astute, considering the twins were as like as two peas in a pod and they had never previously met their host. "You liked the card? It's top of the range of what my company produces, but the candyfloss shops along the Golden Mile still sell ten times more of the 'Have you seen my little Willie?' variety. Even in full make-up, I took a good likeness in those days, but Mayor Bickerstaffe really thought he should have been on the card rather than me!"

There was an awkward silence and then both asked, "But why are we here?"

"Well, you did ask for help, or have you forgotten?"

Both boys were taken aback by their host's reply and another embarrassing silence ensued, which was broken by Blokey's rejoinder.

"Well, you shall go to the ball, as it were, but not directly – nor to the tea dance on the first floor. As I understand it, you need help in writing the history of Cumbria, which you have been tackling by reading boring books. Now, as it happens, I have many contacts who can supply you with all the information you require."

"Yes, you're correct," said Yan. "We've read tens of books and collected data until it's coming out of our ears, but we're no further on!"

"So you have, but you haven't asked a single question to any of the right people. Surely you must have realised from what you've read that archaeologists dig holes and find things, but can't join up the dots."

They both nodded.

"And historians – they read and read and read vellum parchments, paper scrolls and books by the cartload, in Latin, Anglo-Saxon, Danish, Norman French or whatever. They pontificate and write things with deepest sincerity on this or that, then six months later they say something entirely opposite – just like politicians! Truth to tell, you've been basing your research on chaos!"

"He's right," said Tan with a sigh. "That's why we were getting nowhere."

"Turn again, Dick Whittington. But before you do, read this."

Blokey handed over a sheet of paper on which were written the following lines:

'In the Eye of Storms,
Past the Zonnules of Zinn,
Is a land ringed by Wyrms
And the Dragons of Odin.'

"I can see you look perplexed. . . . Well, the land in the verse is Cumbria and her people have over the centuries withstood countless upheavals, invasions and massive political upsets – mostly, and sensibly, they lie low waiting in the eye of the hurricane for these storms to pass. Naturally, there were changes after each deluge, but the people also took those in their stride. And another thing, Cumbria is very much part of the North. Omit what was happening around Cumbria and you will . . . lose sight of the whole plot. Once you grasp those two points, you will begin to understand your county's story in the scheme of things. Now, the first person I would like you to meet is Dubston Skree, who lives in Dubb's Hut near . . . well, here's a map . . . and good luck!"

The boys stared in amazement at the map, but couldn't make head or tail of any of the words and runes written on it. They turned to ask Blokey for more information, but he was no longer in the room – nor anywhere else in the tower, which was by now beginning to sway ever so slightly in the gusts of wind coming down from the north.

The road to Dubb's Hut.

CHAPTER 3 – A TRAIL OF STONE BREADCRUMBS AND ICE

The return trip to Carlisle was a little 'lumpy', due to headwinds and numerous air pockets above the Lake District. Yan and Tan said little, as neither was completely sure of what had occurred earlier that day. True, they now had a map, but not one they could read.

Chibb picked them up in the Austin 7 and, like most trustworthy and totally discreet chauffeurs, listened intently to every word of their conversation. This side of Aikton he could not contain himself any longer.

"Mr Potts knows all about runes and stuff – he's an expert!"

"So, it seems you actually need my help in deciphering some runes and old script?"

Grudgingly, the boys mumbled, "Ye-e-e-es, Mr Potts."

"Show me the map, then" – which they did. "Ah! Interesting . . . even a monkey could decipher this little gem."

"Well, Mr Frank Potts, we're not related to *monkeys*!"

"Quite so! Now, what we have here are two words in Anglo-Saxon, which some people confusingly call Old English, and four others in Scandinavian runes, which, if I'm not mistaken, are Elder Furthark runes and typical of those carved on stone in Scandinavia during the eighth century."

"Well," said Yan, "you learn something new every day."

"The starting point of the journey is at Eiktun, which you know as Aikton – about two and a half miles north-west of here. Then you follow the road to Wicgrtun (Wigton) before heading towards Penrith, which is not named, before turning right at Welton. It's a stiff climb up Warnell, but after that it's mostly all downhill into and through Caldrbekkr (Caldbeck). Crossing over the Glennermackin stream, the road passes by the 'Big Stones' below Carrock Fell. The next feature mentioned is Mungrisdalr, or Mungrisdale, which means 'the valley of St Mungo where the young pigs graze' – indicating that this small valley was at one time filled with oak trees. Pigs like acorns, don't you know! Keep north of the Glennermackin and head south-west for Ceswic (Keswick), which for reasons lost in time was called 'the cheese farm'. Heading south and to the east of Derwent Water, enter Borgar Dalr (Borrowdale) and make for Saerskali (Seatoller) . . . but don't turn off to Seathwaite, which with 140 inches of rain per year is the wettest inhabited village in England. No, head straight on up Honister Pass, which will test the Austin 7's souped-up 696-cc engine to its limit. If you're unlucky, it's an uphill hike of one mile, as the crow flies, and about 800 feet in elevation – depending on where the car conks out. At the quarry don't take the path to the left – to a large cave, rumoured to be called Niflheim – but take the one on the right. It's only a short climb of a couple of hundred feet, but watch out for the ventilation shafts to the slate mines – they're not covered! Then Dubb's Hut is right in front of you. You can't miss it, unless it's misty, which it often is. Did you know your destination used to be a mountain rescue hut before Maester Dubston Skree tarted it up?"

"So, it's boots, ropes and crampons!" said Tan.

"No, not a bit of it – not for sure-footed lads like yourselves," countered Frank Potts rather pointedly, which neither Yan or Tan picked up on.

Dubb's Hut looked, for all the world, just like a windowless shack. It had a single door on which was written in plain English, 'Say the magic word and enter!'

"We're not at Mines of Moria surely . . . I really couldn't cope with Orcs just at this precise moment!" panted Yan.

"Oh, Bollox!" was all his brother could muster – which was a good guess, as a voice from the right ear of a small painted garden gnome on the doorstep confirmed.

"Yes. . . . That's magic! Come in and don't annoy the velociraptors!"

Inside, there were no flesh-eating reptiles, but just a small, bright, shiny stainless-steel room with one button on which was one word: 'Down'. Next to that was an ample supply of heavy-duty paper bags, each inscribed in very bad Latin with '*Sick transit vertigo.*' The button was fake and the lift automatic. Without any warning, except for a burst of high-pitched maniacal laughter and some really awful Muzak, the lift descended at a stomach-churning rate of knots, which would have cheered up no end the manufacturers of a similar conveyance at La Defence in Paris. At least this one was not made of toughened glass and the two near-fainting Hardwicks were spared seeing where they were plunging to.

"Enjoy the ride, boys?" asked Dubston Skree with relish.

When they had recovered, their host, who seemed vaguely familiar, continued.

"We're 500 feet below ground. I have a problem with sunlight – a factor which led me to take up mining as a profession; but then, Blokey has filled you in . . . about that and other things. . . ."

"Not really . . . all we know is that he hinted at your being able to help us . . . to put us on the right track with our history of Cumbria . . . at the beginning, as it were."

"At the beginning," said Dubston, who wore a maroon smoking jacket – which seemed popular with men of his age.

"Well, don't ask the former vicar of St Mary's at Gosforth that question. He still thinks the world is only about 4,000 years old, whereas, as everyone knows, it's nigh on 4 billion years more than that."

"I think that is a little earlier than the beginning we envisaged," the boys volunteered, but there was no stopping Dubston once he had begun.

"True, but you need to have a sense of time. Man and – forgive me – Ovians have only been around for the blink of an eye in geological terms. Hopefully, you don't want to know where the dinosaurs are buried, as there never were any in the county apart from an antiquarian society whose name eludes me for the moment.

"All we have are trilobites, corals, brachiopods, graptolites and gastropods, which can be found in a number of quarries near Kendal, St Bees and Keswick. There are also some fossilised plants near Whitehaven and, of course, vast swathes of carboniferous material – 'coal' to you – along the coast and far out under the Solway Firth and Irish Sea.

"But perhaps we really ought to start your story about the time of the Ice Ages – correct?"

"If you say so . . . but we thought there was only one."

"Where did you go to school? No, there were at least five. The first began 2,400 million years ago and lasted for 500 million years. Another was so severe that the whole earth was almost completely encased in ice and was named the 'Snowball Earth'. There may have been, however, a narrow equatorial region free of glaciers – hence another name, 'Slushball Earth'."

Dubston paused to take a gulp of mead from a bone drinking horn and then continued. "*Homo sapiens*, Neanderthal man and *Ovo bipedus* appeared on the scene in the Rift Valley in Africa between 250,000 and 200,000 years ago. They were very much latecomers – considering the first unicellular life forms preceded them by about 4,000 million years. Well, to cut a long story short, they all left Africa about 150,000 years ago and then spread across the world. The ones who turned left in the Middle East ended up in Europe between the fourth and fifth Ice Ages. Some say the Neanderthals were wiped out around this time – staying too long up north and being trapped by the ice. I'm not convinced by this theory, as I have definitely seen on TV at least twenty or more of these lads lolling about or asleep on the green leather seats in Parliament at Prime Minister's Question Time."

"And the last Ice Age?" yawned Tan, trying to keep awake.

"Yes – that began 110,000 years ago and the last glaciers finally disappeared from Scandinavia sometime just before the beginning of the Mesolithic period – approximately 10,000 BC. At its peak – about 20,000 BC – about sixty per cent of the British Isles was under the ice, which was in places two to three miles thick. Basically, the lowest limit of the ice field began in Galway Bay, spreading south-eastward to Cardigan Bay and then across Southern Wales and England – ending roughly in the Wash. There was so much water bound up in the continental ice sheets that sea level actually dropped by as much as 400 feet. The coastline of Europe was beyond recognition. Here are two maps illustrating what Europe might have looked like in both 20,000 and 13,000 BC. And that", said Dubston Skree, "is the beginning and the end of a trail of stone breadcrumbs and ice. What you need next is someone who can take you further forward and tell you how everyone's ancestors made it up to Cumbria. Perhaps this postcard will help. Blokey asked me to give it to you."

With that, the lights went out, and when they came on again both had a sickening feeling of déjà-vu as the room was quite empty.

20,000 BC				Steppe
	Glacial Ice			Dry Steppe
	Polar Desert			Forest Steppe
	Tundra			Coniferous Woodland

The Ice Age – 20,000 BC.

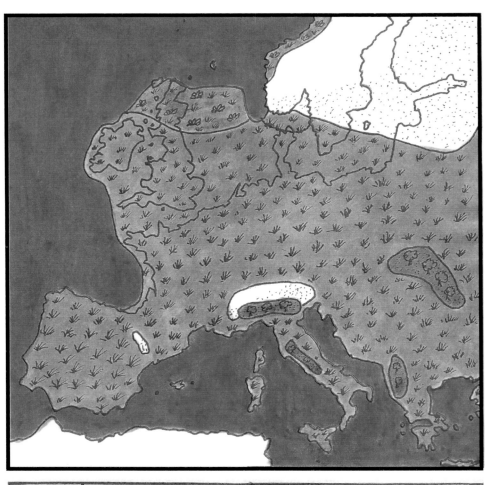

	Glacial Ice		Steppe
	Tundra		Deciduous Woodland

The late glacial period – 13,000 BC.

Genetics

Genes are things
Most tiny, tiny, tiny,
But cows are big
And sometimes mad,
As we've had cause to regret.
You know, of course,
The first mad cow
Was called Margaret.

CHAPTER 4 – GENETICS AND 'STUFF'

In a narrow medieval backstreet behind Paternoster Row and within the sound of Carlisle's cathedral bells was an office on the door of which was written 'Dr Jean d'Allelle, Professor of Human Genetics and Paleoanthropology'.

"It's quite a mouthful," confided Dr d'Allelle to his guests, who were taking tea with him that afternoon, "but all it means is that I study the bones and the chromosomes in them to determine their genetic signature. If other bones with the same signature are found in different sites, it is then possible to establish the migration patterns of tribes travelling across Europe."

"In other words," said Yan with a sense of relief, "you join up the dots."

"Simply but neatly put," reassured the good doctor.

Yan and Tan Hardwick nodded and felt, at last, that they were getting somewhere. Scientific proof seemed now to be replacing airy-fairy speculations and piles of broken pots. Yes, Dr Jean d'Allelle was their man, and they knew all about him as he'd been one of their father's 'guests' at the bunker conference.

Now, Jean d'Allelle, as his name suggests, was of French extraction and his distant ancestor Edward de Lille came to Great Britain quite by mistake in early 1803 with his employer, Madame Marie. Speaking only French, he completely misunderstood the question posed to him by the English manager of Madame Tussaud's waxwork collection, which was . . . "'Eads or tails?"

He replied, "Oui – Edward!"

A coin with the head of Citoyen Capet on it decided Edward's fate. Thus, along with twenty wax heads, including those of Louis Capet himself, his wife, Marie Antoinette, and Monsieur 'Sea-green Incorruptible' Maximilien François Isidore de Robespiere, Edward de Lille crossed the Channel. By May of the same year the fragile fourteen-month truce was over and Edward, along with the rest of Marie Tussaud's entourage, became stranded in Great Britain for the next eleven years.

Edward de Lille prospered, changed his name to d'Allelle and became a loyal subject of George III. His great-great-great-great-grandson, Jean, also a great lover of this country – especially of Cumbria – had one fatal flaw. The fickle finger of fate had endowed him, for reasons beyond comprehension, with a blind spot – i.e. an unaccountable dislike of Yorkshire and its inhabitants, whom he called 'ticks', rather than their usual colloquial name, tykes.

As a result of this aberration, he had over the years lost a few teeth and gained a lifetime's ban from entering that county ever again. Undeterred, he persisted in repeating with relish the story of Dr Johnson (the dictionary inventor) and an unidentified Frenchman. The good doctor, or so the story went, had advised the Frenchman as follows:

"You must never ask an Englishman if he comes from Yorkshire, because if he does, he will almost certainly tell you; and if he doesn't there really is no need to insult him!"

The recounting of this story is of no great consequence whatsoever, except that it does explain the reason why Dr Jean d'Allelle asked Yan and Tan Hardwick the following question:

"You don't happen to come from Yorkshire, do you?"

With a shake of their heads, the ice was broken and Dr d'Allelle smiled.

"Now, at the end of the last Ice Age – approximately 22,000 years ago – there were only five refuges for *Homo sapiens* et al. below the Northern European glacial wall and polar desert. These small communities of hunter-gatherers were spread from the west to the east – just below the tree line – from South-Western France to the Ukraine. Gradually, the world became warmer and wetter. The icefields began to retreat and grasslands gradually spread across Europe. With the grass came the herds of deer, wild cattle and a host of other herbivores. Behind them came the carnivores – some of which walked on two legs. With an increased intake of protein, the small tribes of men increased in numbers. Individually they became healthier and stronger. Collectively they followed the herds and migrated northward and westward. The first ones to venture forth were those from South-Western France. They started to move around 14,000 BC, but the tribes in Eastern Europe, where the global climate changes lagged behind those in the warmer west, began their migration a little later – around 11,000 BC."

Dr d'Allelle paused to let this information sink in.

"But how do you know all this?" enquired Yan.

"The tools of my trade are two in number," Dr d'Allelle continued. "The first involves radiocarbon dating, which enables the fairly precise estimation of the age of any material – whether animal or vegetable – which has lived or grown in the past. Invented by Dr Willard Libby sometime in the 1940s, the dating process is now much more accurate. Sadly, nothing is perfect and one has to accept that accuracy in determining the exact date when the owner of a particular bone lived becomes less precise the further back in time one goes. Nevertheless, it is possible to say that a bone (and therefore its human owner) lived 20,000, 10,000, 5,000 or 2,000 years ago and so on. As a result of this scientific discovery, archaeologists have been jumping backwards through hoops for decades, as they are able to confirm with a degree of accuracy the date of their findings. The same archaeologists are less than enthusiastic about the second tool or weapon in my armamentarium – DNA analysis, which I hinted at earlier. The same bones which can be dated using carbon 14 can also reveal information based on the genetic material they contain."

Dr d'Allelle paused, realising the boys were now looking a tad weary. TMI, or 'too much information', was setting in.

"Perhaps we should take a break. Come back tomorrow and we can continue where we have just left off. There are plenty of interesting things to see in Carlisle – the Carvings in Room 22 on the second floor of the keep in the castle would be right up your street – or should I say Castle Street? They reveal, in cartoon-like images on stone and wood, the history of the Borders from the twelfth to the sixteenth century – as seen through the eyes of the simple, illiterate common men who carved them and who could not pass on in any other way the story of what was happening all around them at the time."

The next day, refreshed and attentive, the Hardwick boys listened to Dr Jean d'Allelle as he continued his revelations concerning the distant past.

"We are who and what we are – or, to a lesser extent, who our ancestors were – because of detailed biological codes, hard-wired into the matrix of each and every cell in our bodies. These instructions are laid down in twenty-three pairs of chromosomes!"

"Does that go for sheep as well?" asked Tan.

"No, they have fifty-two in total as opposed to a human's forty-six."

"There, I told you so!" whispered Yan to his brother, grinning from ear to ear.

"Size isn't everything. Garden snails have fifty-four, dogs seventy-eight, hedgehogs ninety and goldfish 100."

Totally deflated, Tan slumped back into the comfortable embrace of the good doctor's armchair.

"In turn, chromosomes are made up of thousands of smaller data units, called genes, which are themselves composed of four basic nitrogen-containing organic chemicals or bases, arranged in specific patterns in their hundreds of thousands!"

"Little fleas have smaller fleas upon their backs to bite 'em, and littler fleas have even smaller fleas – and so on ad infinitum!" murmured Yan, recalling a misremembered rhyming doggerel, half-learnt long ago.

"Well, close enough, I suppose, but did you know or even suspect that the sum total of paired bases in one cell of a human being is 3,079,843,747!"

"Does that go for sheep too?" blurted out Tan.

"Sheep! I haven't the faintest idea! And what's this obsession with bloody sheep!"

"Don't mind him, Doctor. He's got a thing about . . . film stars," reassured Yan, who simultaneously shot a dagger-like glance at his brother.

"Film Stars?"

"'Fraid so . . . but, if you haven't seen the film *Babe*, you wouldn't understand."

Dr d'Allelle paused, took in a deep breath, struggled to regain his train of thought and returned to what for him should have been a relatively simple explanation. "We are about to come to the really interesting bit – the part about haplogroups. These are specific collections of genes, handed on by each parent to their offspring . . . and . . . in turn handed down from their parents before them. There is obviously some selection as to what is handed down, but it is sometimes possible to identify a common ancestry from earlier generations – sometimes dating back many thousands of years. It is not possible, however, to roll out a genetic chart many tens of thousands of years long and identify each and every ancestor or tribal/national group from the past."

"Really? And I thought that was exactly what a number of commercial genetically orientated firms claimed they could do!" Yan countered.

"Well, they can't. However, a much more important discovery has come to light, as by identifying specific haplogroup signatures in the bones of long-dead hunter-gatherers it is possible to track the movements of tribal groups across continents tens of thousands of years ago."

"Now, that really is interesting and I expect the archaeologists were even more pleased to learn that," Yan added.

"Far from it! These discoveries have put a cat amongst the pigeons. Many archaeologists whose erroneous theories concerning tribal migrations had gone unchallenged for decades now find themselves almost surplus to requirement!" After a brief pause, Dr d'Allelle continued. "At this point, I want to show you four maps to clarify everything we have been discussing. Two are of Doggerland – a land finally submerged under the North Sea around 5000 BC – showing how, with the rising sea levels, its size gradually shrank between 16,000 and 7000 BC; and the other two illustrate some important migration patterns.

"Probably the first migration that ever occurred, and certainly the first that was plotted, is that of the haplogroup Vera, or Velda. Simple names are often used rather than the official unmemorable alphanumeric codes – and this group travelled from South-Western France to Southern England and Belgium around 14,000 BC. The second haplogroup – Ruy, or R1b-13 and Rb1-10 – travelled from South-Western France up to England, Ireland and North-Western France in the Mesolithic period (10,000 to 5000 BC). As you can see, the most northerly destination of this group on the map appears to be Cumbria, and it so happens that the first proven postglacial evidence of human habitation in the county was found at Kirkhead Cave, near Ulverston, The bones in that cave have been dated at between 11,400 and 10,800 BC, which is close enough."

"Now we are finally getting somewhere," said Tan. "Please tell us more about the cat amongst the pigeons."

"I'm afraid I can only offer you a clue – 'The Celts' – and a postcard, which arrived this morning. On it is the picture and tale of a six-legged cat. For any information about Celts, cats and pigeons, I'm afraid that you will have to talk to Bangalore Locksley, a former colleague of mine, who now lives in Cumwhitton, which in Brythonic Celtic is 'Cymryton' and means 'The village of the Cymyr'.

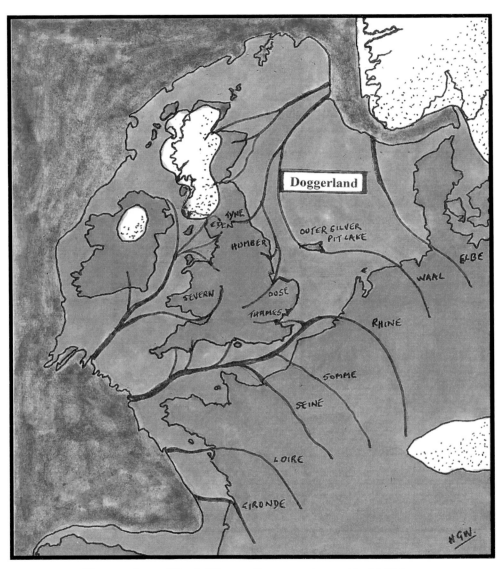

The coastline of North-Western Europe, today and in 16,000 BC.

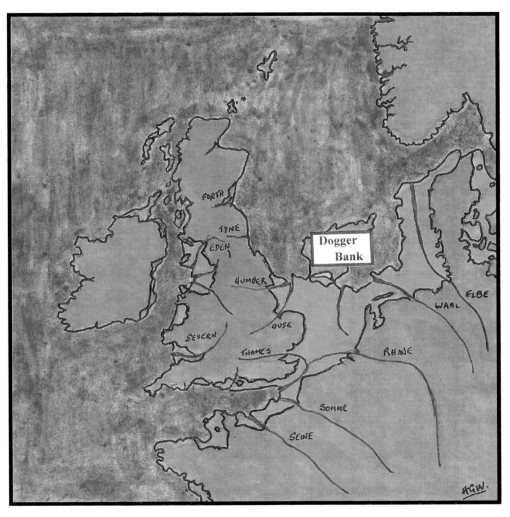

The coastline of North-Western Europe, today and in 7000 BC.

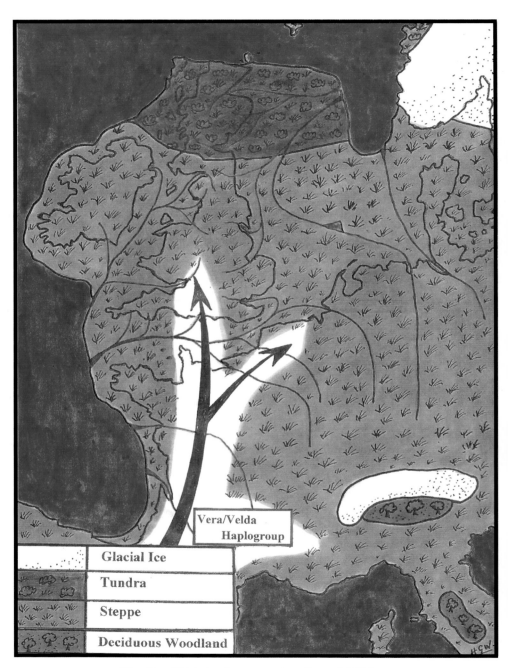

The Vera/Velda haplogroup migration – 14,000 BC.

Legend:
- Glacial Ice
- Tundra
- Steppe
- Deciduous Woodland

Vera/Velda
Haplogroup

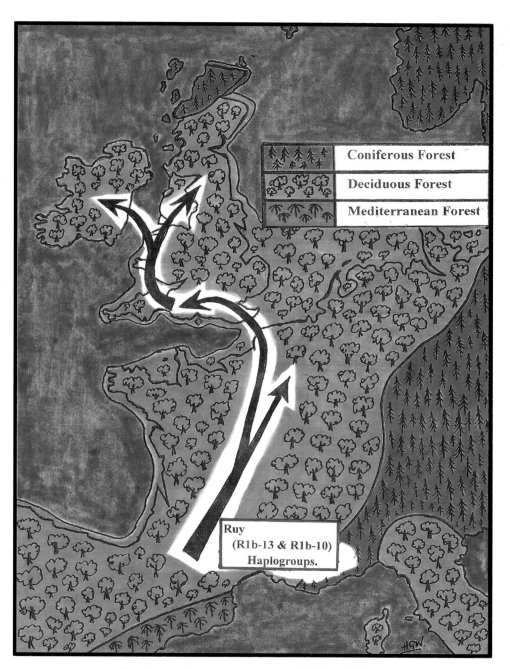

The Ruy haplogroup migration – 10,000–5000 BC.

The Cat with Six Legs

The cat with six legs stumbled on.
He didn't kna his lettas
And ni-body told him to his face
That four rather than six was betta!

His coat was red with bits of green –
He look'd a propa mess.
And then one day he met a zebra
In a bright-blue stripey dress.

They married then and there.
It was monumentally 'Quartzan'!
And that is why we have today
The thing we all call tartan.

('Quartzan' is an untranslatable expression used by Debra the zebra on her wedding day.)

CHAPTER 5 – A CAT AMONGST THE PIGEONS

Cumwhitton is a small village about three miles to the south-east of Carlisle. It boasts a few houses, a church, and a pub called The Six-Legged Cat, which was where the somewhat clandestine meeting with Mr Bangalore Locksley was to take place. D'Allelle's instructions had been simple. Both Hardwick boys were to carry a copy of the *Cumberland News* and to look for a balding middle-aged man with a small *chou-fleur* in the left lapel of his red corduroy smoking jacket.

A question – "Are you Bangalore Locksley?" – was also part of the opening gambit and was delivered by Yan with panache and elan.

"Of course not!" – which was the expected response. This, as it happened, was followed by "Actually, I'm a geneticist, like d'Allelle, living incognito and trying to evade agents from the Archaeologists Anonymous hit squad. My real name is Dominus Nullius Axillae (my father was a Latin scholar), but you can call me DNA for short. You're here to get me off the hook, I hope."

"No" was the muted chorus of denial. "D'Allelle sent us here to learn all about cats, pigeons and possibly Celts, which for all we know may just be a wild goose chase."

"You may sneer, but this is serious stuff. We can't talk here – too dangerous by far."

With that he retrieved two double-barrelled shotguns from behind the bar, then ushered us through the snug and out by the back door. En route to his hideout – Quartzan Cottage – he bagged two tramps, an unlucky poacher and an innocent hitch-hiker.

"Four assassins down – we should be safe for a while at least."

Yan and Tan exchanged looks of disbelief and wondered if before the afternoon was out they too might be classified as assassins.

The atmosphere in Quartzan Cottage was much more relaxed. DNA brought in a pot of Earl Grey and a freshly cooked date-and-walnut cake, which they all tucked into. Then, after lighting a medium-sized Cuban cigar with the glowing red tip of a poker, their host, visibly at ease, recommenced the discourse which d'Allelle had so abruptly ended.

"I assume my colleague has already told you about the 10,000 years of migrations from South-Western France to Northern Europe and the British Isles. Good, but did he mention the name of the nation which undertook that trek? I think you inferred that he had. Well, the Celts, or perhaps a better name might be the proto-Celts, who were responsible for repopulating North-Western Europe, were my discovery – or at least identifying them as such was – and a lot of good it did me too! You see, what had been previously taken as gospel I unceremoniously and irrevocably debunked. It was I who put the cat amongst the pigeons and, as a result, they sent Morgan Klegg to deal with me."

"And he was or is?" asked Yan.

"An employee of the Ashmolean Museum and an enforcer for Archaeologists Anonymous."

The phone rang and DNA offered a one-sentence response to the caller.

"Yes, Dr Killjoy, I have taken my tablets today."

There was a brief pause, while our host, with sleight of hand, downed four triangular vivid-green pills.

"Where was I? Yes, the Celts! According to Herodotus, the Father of History, the Celts lived in a region about halfway up the River Danube, which, he had been reliably informed, sprang from the Pyrenees. This put the Celtic homeland squarely bang in Central Europe. Despite a host of other ancient writers, navigators and soldiers, like Strabo, Himilco and Julius Caesar, who had personal knowledge of the Celts and their homeland, which they declared straddled the western end of the Pyrenees, the views of 'Father' Herodotus stuck. Various notables over the years repeated and expanded on this myth. Prominent amongst them was Edward Lhuyd, a Welsh linguist and antiquarian, who became keeper of the Ashmolean between 1691 and 1709. The nineteenth-century French anatomist and surgeon, Pierre Paul Broca, after whom the Broca's area in the left posterior inferior frontal gyrus is named, was also an anthropologist and he believed the Celts or Gauls arrived in France from Central Europe."

"Riveting stuff, DNA," murmured Tan under his breath, which the ever alert doctor heard.

"Thank you for those few kind words, Mr Hardwick. Well, I did not go along with the old theory, especially when the scientific facts proved the origin of the paths of migration. Then other evidence came to light – that the dead centre of all these waves of migration was a region on the west coast of France, where, around 2000 BC, the Celtic tongue was thought to have developed. Putting two and two together (or was it three and three – the migration patterns, the genetic analyses and the origin of the Celtic tongue?), it seemed obvious that the Celts had originated in South-Western France. So I published an article."

"Makes sense to us," said the boys.

"Well, it didn't to the archaeologists. All those years of digging up bones, pots and whatever in Central Europe – all those eminent professors teaching their students and all those books – had been for nothing! I was asked to reconsider my opinions and retract all that I had publicly proclaimed, but I couldn't and wouldn't, so they put a contract out on me. Now you know the whole story."

Truth is sometimes stranger than fiction, and on occasion both are intertwined. Yan and Tan left Cumwhitton with a lot on their minds. Before heading back to Wiggonby, they dropped in to see Dr Jean d'Allelle, who was in the process of hurriedly packing a suitcase.

"You've heard, then," he said with sadness.

"Heard what?"

"They shot him. DNA is dead. I'm off to France, to a place where no one will ever find me."

"Where exactly?" asked Tan absent-mindedly.

Whether they did or not, as the barman in *Irma la Douce* was fond of saying, that is another story – and one which is not part of the ongoing saga of Yan and Tan Hardwick.

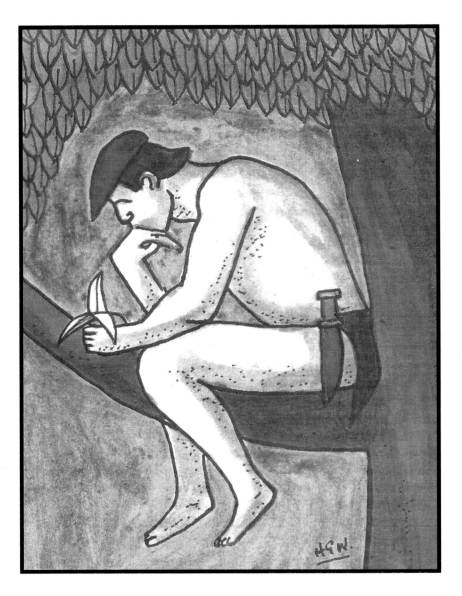

Deep Thought at Lowca.

CHAPTER 6 – MARE OF THE CELTS

Meanwhile 'back at the ranch' in Wiggonby, Yan and Tan were not happy – doubly so because of the demise of DNA and the realisation that their research had literally come to an apparent dead end.

With uncanny timing a solution in the form of yet another postcard arrived by the midday post. Its words were cryptic and few.

'Deep Thought at Lowca.'

"Very drole! Who sent the card?" chortled Tethra Hardwick.

"We suspect, but don't know for sure – not yet, Fatha."

"You must realise that Deep Thought is not his real name. It was Carvetius Brock, reader of Celtic studies and all-round good egg at one of the Oxbridge colleges. On retirement, like many with the instinct of a salmon, he returned home, which in his case was to Lowca. His family, way back in 1800, set up an ironworks near the mouth of Lowca Beck, about three miles north of Whitehaven. By the 1850s and under new management, the engineering works were producing locomotives, but the future of Lowca's factory at Parton lay beneath the surface – in the form of extensive deposits of coal. By 1911 a factory, based on German technology, began to produce synthetic chemicals from the black gold – chemicals which would be vital in the coming world war. However, on 16 August 1915 a German submarine, U-24, surfaced off Parton and shelled the factory – killing one dog. The bombardment of Hartlepool by German surface ships in the previous December had resulted in 130 dead, but Parton avoided such a butcher's bill by the act of a Swedish engineer called Oscar Olsen. He opened an exhaust valve, causing an enormous plume of flame to erupt above the works. Believing a direct hit had been achieved, U-24 submerged and left the scene."

"Why did you say Carvetius Brock was called Deep Thought?"

"It was on account of his posture while tackling profound mental problems. A local reporter caught him on camera in such a pose and immediately compared him to Rodin's bronze, *The Thinker*. It wasn't long before a photograph of Brock appeared in *The Star*, and the name stuck."

"Fascinating as all that is, can he help us?"

"Without a doubt, he can," reassured their father, "but you'd better be quick, as according to the local TV he's currently up a tree in a local park, dressed as Tarzan in a cloth cap and refusing to come down! You'll easily spot him – he's eating a banana."

"There's familiar ring about all these experts," mused Tan. "They're all a bit eccentric . . . if that's the correct psychiatric term."

"If he's very adamant about not coming down . . . just say you've got Tethra's photographs!"

Sure enough, Carvetius Brock was up a tree – deep in thought and eating a banana.

"Perhaps Dad's theory about evolution has more than a grain of truth," Yan confided in his brother before passing through the police cordon surrounding a *Prunus zanzar* in Jubilee Park.

"Good afternoon. My name is Yan Hardwick and our father, Tethra, sent us."

"Yes, but I am still not coming down. It was a very bad idea for our ancestors to vacate the trees . . . they were much happier up there. I've thought about it and that's that."

"Well, the fire brigade have a really big chainsaw which they haven't had a chance to use . . . yet."

"Don't care!"

"Nothing whatever will change your mind?"

"Nothing!"

"Not even these photographs of you and—"

"I'm coming down this very minute" – which he did with alacrity.

"You've got a way with words, young man. Ever thought of joining the force?" asked Inspector Truncheon-Whackem, who had more gold braid and silver acorns on his cap and epaulettes than General Douglas MacArthur. "Take Mr Brock home and sort him out before the men in white coats arrive."

Hot Bovril works wonders and hot Bovril with brandy is even better. Within two shakes of a lamb's tail Carvetius Brock was in a mellow co-operative frame of mind and more than willing to pour out his knowledge to his attentive audience. In fact, it almost seemed as if he had expected to meet the boys.

"By the Iron Age – around 800 BC – the whole of Britain, apart from the Pictish lands above what is now referred to as the Highland line, was inhabited entirely by twenty-four Celtic tribes. They had all originally come up from Southern Gaul during the Neolithic period around 4000 BC, but the proto- or early Celts had made the journey long before that. Initially they spoke the same tongue – Goidelic Celtic – but around 1000 BC another version, Brythonic Celtic, came into existence. Of course nobody knows why this happened, and the difference was, more or less, related to pronunciation. The former Goidelic Celtic is referred to as Q-Celtic and was spoken in three major regions – in Ireland as Gaeilige, or Irish Gaelic; in the west of Scotland as Gaidhlig, or Scottish Gaelic; and on the Isle of Man it went by the name of Gaeig/Gailik, or Manx. Brythonic/Brithonic Celtic, known as P-Celtic, was the tongue of three major Celtic regions on the mainland. In Wales we know it as Cymraeg, or Welsh, whereas in Cornwall/Devon it went by the name of Kernow/Kernowek, or Cornish. In the third general region – England and Southern Scotland – there were five sub-varieties, of which the most well-known was Cumbric, the future language of the Celtic Kingdom of Strathclyde, a ninety-by-fifty-mile strip of land running north to south from Glasgow to Penrith, sandwiched between Northumbria in the east and Galwyddel in the south-west.

"There would also be two other regions in Europe which would eventually adopt Brythonic Celtic as their native tongue. The first was Brittany, which like the whole of Gaul initially spoke Goidelic Celtic. Then, in AD 383, General Magnus Maximus, the military commander of Britannia, made his play for the throne of the Western Empire. He invaded Gaul – taking with him his army, of which more than a few apparently came from Cornwall. Maximus might well have achieved his objective, but he was greedy. Trying to win both thrones and reunite the empire under his command, he lost everything. Some of his troops remained on the continent and settled in Brittany, and that is why the Celtic tongue of the Bretons sounds so much like that spoken in Cornwall and Wales. The second region was Galicia, on the north-western tip of Spain, to which in the fifth and sixth centuries there were seaborne migrations from Brittany – hence the reason why Brythonic Celtic took root there.

"And what happened to all the other Celtic languages in Europe, you might ask – Goidelic Celtic of Gaul; Lepotic of Switzerland and Northern Italy; Celtibrian of Aragon and Castile; as well as the original Galician of Galicia, Asturias and Portugal? Well, they went the way of the dodo – into extinction."

Carvetius Brock paused for a moment and waited for questions, of which there were none.

"Now, at this point, I need to tell you about the misuse of two words, with regard to spoken Celtic languages, as it has caused massive confusion over the years. It's a bit like the habit of some 'historians' who still persist in referring to Anglo-Saxon as Old English – as if the latter was Modern English with a hint of dialect and a strong Somerset accent. The first word is Brythonic, or Brithonic, which has been referred to as the language of the Britons – almost totally denying the existence of the Celts and inferring that they had insidiously been replaced by another variety of ancient British Peoples – the Britons. The second is Cumbric – the Brythonic Celtic tongue of Strathclyde – which some 'historians' refer to as the language spoken by Cumbrians – hence almost causing Strathclyde to be thought of in some readers' minds as either Cumberland or Cumbria.

"You look a bit overwhelmed, boys. It's time for a break and a little snack."

So, without much ado, out came a side of ham, a crusty loaf of bread, some rum butter, mustard, apple sauce and enough mead and ale to refloat RMS *Titanic*.

"You don't get scran like this in trees, Mr Brock," mumbled Tan with a mouth half full of ham.

"No . . . but then again, I really didn't intend to stay up there for long. Mrs Rhudd, my housekeeper, got all this lot in while I was entertaining Lowca. I have a reputation to keep up – academics are eccentric, or didn't you know?

"Now, where were we? Ah, yes, just before Julius Caesar's Roman legions appeared on the scene – in 55 BC. By that time the Celtic tribes in Cumbria had achieved all the characteristics of an Iron Age culture.

50

This term, like that of Stone Age and Bronze Age, had been devised in the nineteenth century by archaeologists. Basically, the developmental stages of peoples were aligned to the principle material of their tools and weapons. It was a broad-based classification, which made no direct reference to any other advances in their culture – such as pottery, art, jewellery, religion, social structure, buildings, etc. Over the decades more and more artefacts have been unearthed and a wider understanding of ancient peoples has led to subdivisions of the original classifications – hence terms like New Stone Age and Middle Iron Age began to be used. By 55 BC, Britain was in the Late Iron Age, when the 'warrior culture' was well and truly established – along with techniques of warfare such as using lightweight chariots and hill forts.

"Stone circles, like Castlerigg, Swinside, and Long Meg and her Daughters, had been built much earlier – in the New Stone Age, between 5000 and 2500 BC – all down the west coast of Europe, but not exclusively so. They were still in use for religious and social gatherings, astronomical and seasonal calculations and, without a doubt, 'rock concerts'.

"Large groups of peoples collected together in tribes, which had leaders and a hierarchy based primarily on the warrior status of tribal members. Obviously, other than warfare and to a lesser extent mining and metalworking, the main preoccupation of these peoples was agriculture – crop production and animal husbandry. In fact, life and the seasons revolved around food production, which is why, for the most part, the people lived in small farming communities, grouped in families, living in up to ten round houses per village. There is still a great deal of discussion relating to whether larger settlements, such as towns, existed, or if each tribal region had a capital. In Northern Cumbria, it has been suggested that Carlisle or Penrith served such a function. However, if regional centres did exist, they may only have been used as sites for large-scale gatherings, where tribal leaders and their people discussed important matters. Trading/bartering between tribal groups and nations also occurred, but without the use of money. The exchange of goods helped to spread new technologies, information and social customs as well as exposing potential customers to new foods and beverages. However, it was generally understood that merchants, especially those from powerful kingdoms, were probably spying on the lands they were trading in.

"So, which tribes, you might ask, lived in Cumbria around 55 BC? In the north were the Carvetii and in the south the Setanti. Both belonged to a confederation of which the Brigantes were the dominant tribe. The Parisi – a tribe inhabiting a region just north of the Humber – were also part of this large grouping. There was probably a fair degree of independence within each of the smaller tribes, who basically came together to face serious external military threats – such as the Romans. Then the ruler of the Brigantes would assume the prime role of commanding the armies of the confederacy.

"He or she would also have had a role to play in terms of diplomacy, when agreements and non-aggression pacts could be arranged. The Romans called such states which were peaceful, co-operative and willing to collaborate with them 'client states', and for a time, under Queen Cartimandua, the Brigantian confederacy was such. But that would be all in the future, because the Romans did not venture into the north of Britain for another 100 years or more – well after Gaius Julius Caesar had wetted his feet in the salt water along the shore of Kent."

"I am impressed," said Tan, who had not fallen asleep – mainly because, for the first time, an expert was talking at length and directly about the county.

"Now, the map showing the tribes of Cumbria – the Carvetii and the Setanti – is it accurate?" asked Yan.

"I think it is, but there are bound to be others who won't agree. In my opinion the Carvetii were a tribe who inhabited the Solway Plain to the north and south of our 'Brown Sea', the Solway, and also both down the west coast and up the Eden Valley. The Setanti probably lived in the south of the county as well as in North Lancashire. As for the central Lake District, who knows, but boundaries for all these tribal areas must have been related to geographic features like rivers, shorelines and mountain ridges."

"And what about the towns?" asked Tan.

"Your Mr Frank Potts has sent me his first toponymic map, which might be of help. He believes that if the current name of any town/village in the county can be directly associated to the Brythonic Celtic language, then Brythonic Celts must have lived there at one time. So, according to Mr Potts' map, the Carvetii lived in what we now call Carlisle, Cargo, Drumburgh, Eaglesfield, Glenridding, Penrith and Penruddock."

"But the Setanti only had Barrow-in-Furness!" blurted out Tan between guffaws.

52

"There is a flaw or rather an important consideration to be taken into account with regard to Frank's map. It only shows what it shows and is a bit like what you can see through holes in wallpaper. Yes, these place names are Brythonic in origin, but the absence of others does not mean that the Celts didn't live in settlements all over the county. Clearly they must have, but later national groups renamed what they wanted to – in their own tongue. Keep watching this space – I think Frank has more maps up his sleeve."

"I see on the map some of the rivers, lakes and mountains are in colour, whereas many others are merely outlined in black and are unnamed. Has Mr Potts used this form of identification to denote those features which have an irrefutable Celtic connection?"

"Well spotted! Now, you are probably wondering if this map is based on contemporary written evidence – Celtic script on a roll of vellum. Well, the answer is no. The Celts did have a written language, but they seldom used it. Even those who later learned to speak and write in Latin rarely used their own script. They were a very secretive people who did not like to commit to writing anything about themselves, and wrote absolutely nothing about their religion. Perhaps writing was only used as part of religious ceremonies – and then shortly afterwards the evidence was incinerated to maintain the secrets of the gods. Who knows?"

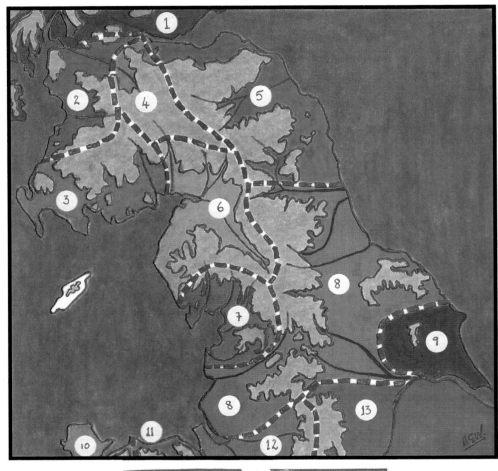

1	Caledonian Confederacy	7	Setanti
2	Damnonii	8	Brigantes
3	Novantae	9	Parisi
4	Selgovae	10	Ordivices
5	Votadini	11	Deceangli
6	Carvetii	12	Cornovi
		13	Coritani

The Celtic tribes of Northern Britannia.

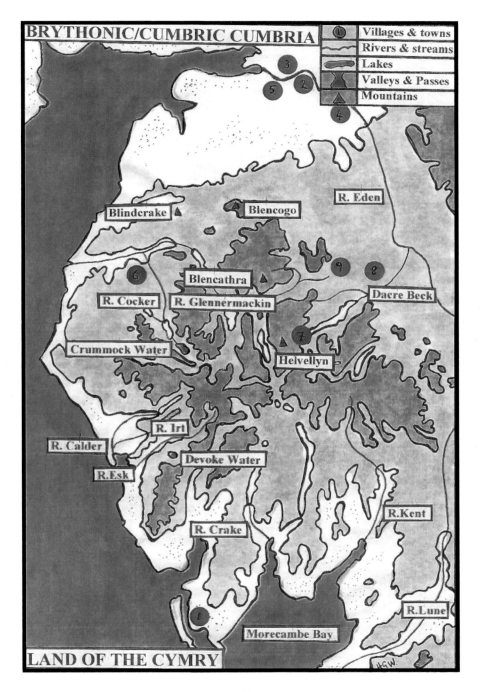

BRYTHONIC/CUMBRIC CUMBRIA

	Villages & towns
	Rivers & streams
	Lakes
	Valleys & Passes
	Mountains

R. Eden

Blindcrake

Blencogo

Blencathra

R. Cocker

R. Glennermackin

Dacre Beck

Crummock Water

Helvellyn

R. Irt

R. Calder

Devoke Water

R.Esk

R.Kent

R. Crake

R.Lune

Morecambe Bay

LAND OF THE CYMRY

SINISTER DEXTER
CANIS BELLI
NUMERUS BARCIORUM
TIBERIENSIUM

CHAPTER 7 – SINISTER DEXTER – DOG OF WAR

"There are an awful lot books about the Romans, but not much about the ancient Cumbrians," bemoaned Yan.

"Brythonic-speaking Celts of the Carvetii and Setanti tribes – don't you mean, young Master Hardwick? Or so tree-hugging Deep Thought would have you to say!" Tan retorted.

"It's my impression that, apart from a few merchants and collaborators, the majority of the locals kept their heads down for the full 350 years the Romans were lording it over them. According to 'Fussy' Potts' second map, they didn't leave behind much of an impression by way of place names in the county. All I can see on it are the Rivers Ellen and Derwent and, of course, Derwent Water – but I'm not so sure about the Eden."

"Well, there are still lots of ruined buildings, baths, roads and, of course, Hadrian's Wall. Tan, you're beginning to sound like the Judaean People's Front, or were they the People's Front of Judaea?"

The shuffling sound of Chibb Swaledale's slippers on the stone floor announced his arrival.

"Another postcard. . . . This one's from a Colonel W. Robinson of Mowdy Castle near Kirkbride."

On the card was a brightly coloured miniature of a terrier on what appeared to be a medallion, beneath which was written in imperial script:

'SINISTER DEXTER
CANIS BELLI
NUMERUS BARCIORUM
TIBERIENSIUM'

"And what do you make of that, young sirs?"

"All I can pick out is 'dog's belly' and 'lots of barking'," said Tan. "I'm fed up with this library and am up for a trip to the Moricambe Bay Riviera."

"Colonel Windermere Robinson's the name – bit of a mouthful, but you can call me Windy. The boys at Sandy's called me that – perfectly acceptable. G & T time! Want one?"

Although a tad brusque, the Colonel was a cheery sort and made the boys welcome. Minutes later, sitting on the terrace above the wide expanse of Moricambe Bay, the trio took in the view.

"Kirkbride, up the Wampool, is to our left – used to be the main Roman supply port for the forts between Carlisle and Moresby in the time of Trajan – and a fine-looking fellow he was too! Mind you, it wasn't much of a port – only one shallow-draught boat a day could make it up the eight-mile channel from Grune Point near Skinburness to Portus Trucculensis, and then only at high water. Those little boats came all that way from Chester – amazing! Get stuck out there at low water, and the mud and quicksand would do for you. They had pilots, of course – the boys of the Numerus Barciorum Tiberiensium – 'bargemen from the Tiber'."

"Ah, yes, the medallion!" chirped in Tan.

"Thought you'd like it. Sinister Dexter – 'Left Right' in Latin – was the mascot of that mob of irregulars. The real brass medallion landed on this very terrace a couple of years ago, when a shard of lightning hit an unexploded bomb in the trees near the beck. There used to be an RAF Coastal Command training base over there – just this side of Silloth, where the Oiks used to learn to fly bombers. They managed to crash so many of the Bristol Beauforts, Avro Ansons, Blackburn Bothas and especially Lockheed Hudsons into the sea near Cockleggies lighthouse, just south of Silloth, that the locals called the area Hudson Bay. Well, for a short time they also 'taught' them to drop live bombs into Moricambe Bay – hence the medallion. We had a host of archybolockogists here for a while and I put them straight on a few matters – used to teach military history at Sandy's, don't you know?"

"Sandy's?"

"Sandhurst. Your father rang – said you needed a few pointers, which I'm more than glad to do . . . as it's very boring up here. I like to take potshots at the wildfowlers, which only seems fair . . . but it's the wrong time of year."

"How did the Romans end up here?" Yan enquired.

"Clau-Clau-Claudius, as Robert Graves nicknamed Emperor Tiberius Claudius Drusus Nero Germanicus, wanted to make a name for himself and invaded Britain in AD 43 at the head of four legions and four elephants. I think he would have been quite happy just holding on to the south of England, but warring tribes on the borders of his fledgling province drew his legions ever deeper north into the island.

"It was in AD 51 that Caratacus, leader of the Catuvellauni in Mid-Wales, was defeated by Governor Publius Ostorius Scapula. He fled to the Brigantes tribe, hoping for sanctuary, but Queen Cartimandua, ruler of that Roman client state, duly handed him over to the Governor. Taken to Rome in chains, Caratacus made a stirring speech to the senate and appealed directly to the Emperor Claudius to reverse his death penalty – which he granted. Meanwhile, back in Northern Britannia, Venutius, Cartimandua's husband and alleged member of the Carvetii tribe, was less than happy with the treatment Caratacus had received at his wife's hands. He was even less pleased when she took up with his armour bearer, Vellocatus. Divorce, civil war and two revolts against Rome followed. The embittered divorcees, however, disappeared without trace from the pages of history around AD 69.

"Further revolts followed and – as Gnaeus Julius Agricola, Governor of Britannia put it in a letter to Emperor Vespasian in AD 78 – 'The Brigantes really are revolting.' But, as Agricola was also an accomplished General, he promptly defeated the northern tribes in AD 79, annexing the Brigantian homelands in the process.

"Then, after thoroughly crushing the Celtic armies in Southern Scotland in AD 82 and the Picts at Mons Graupius in Perthshire the following year, Agricola was of the opinion he could probably mop up the rest of Caledonia and then do the same in Hibernia (Ireland) with the aid of IX Hispana and XX Valeria Victrix legions.

"Domitian was now on the throne, following the death of his brother Titus (both were sons of Vespasian). He really wasn't interested in conquering the British Isles and, more to the point, Agricola was getting a bit too cocky. So after six years as Governor – two years longer than most governors served anywhere in the empire – Agricola was recalled to Rome in AD 83 to a very quiet reception, to retirement and, according to his family, to poison administered on the instructions of Domitian ten years later."

After a slight pause, 'Windy' Robinson returned to his account of the early days of the Roman occupation of the north of Britannia, but not before Yan broke the ice with "So, it was all quiet of the northern front for a while after Agricola left?"

"Agricola had, apart from building a number of forts in the pacified lands of Southern Scotland, set in motion a plan to erect a loose defensive line between the Solway and the Tyne."

"I thought Hadrian did that!"

"Hadrian completed what would turn out to be phase two, which lasted from AD 117 to 138. Agricola's phase one, which began in the early eighties, was sound, but nowhere near as formidable. He began with the construction of two large turf-and-timber forts to guard the river crossings over the Eden and Tyne – one at Carlisle and the other at Corbridge – and connected them with a substantial military road, which then formed the 'Stanegate Line'. Between these forts were two others – one at Nether Denton, east of Carlisle, and the other at Vindolanda, west of Corbridge. Additionally, the gap between Carlisle and Bowness-on-Solway was covered by seven smaller forts. This should have been more than adequate, but all military planning falls down when the first blows of conflict are struck – which in this case were in AD 100, when the Brigantes revolted again – soon to be followed by an invasion by Picts in AD 105, between Corbridge and the east coast. Finally, around AD 117 the IX Hispana disappeared – probably ambushed and destroyed by a mixed force of Brigantes and Picts somewhere north of the Stanegate Line, most likely in revenge for its participation in the butchery of the Celts and Picts in the campaigns of Agricola. The effect on the new emperor, Hadrian, echoed that of Augustus's loss of the XVII, XVIII and XIX Legions in the Teutoburg Forest in AD 9.

"Hadrian travelled to the Border region to assess the situation personally and then drew up a new plan, which involved the construction of a permanent line of defence seventy-three miles in length between Bowness-on-Solway and Wallsend. It would have around twenty major forts, eighty fortlets or mile castles and about 160 turrets between the mile castles. Initially constructed in turf and timber, it is estimated that between 1 million and 2 million pines or firs were felled. Later, the wooden structure was replaced by stone defence works constructed with nine-inch-cubed limestone and sandstone blocks – possibly in the tens of millions.

"Cumbria would later be defended by a further seven forts between Bowness and Ravenglass – all built in the turf-and-timber pattern with a continuous palisade sixty miles long to prevent any outflanking of Hadrian's Wall by seaborne invasions.

"The troops defending these structures were auxiliary units from all over the empire, but mostly from North-West Europe. They would consist of cavalry, infantry, part-mounted infantry and some irregular units. A total of around 15,000 soldiers would man the wall, with approximately one-third being cavalry. In the twenty-odd forts across the whole of Cumbria there would have been around 5,500 troops, of which – again – one-third would be cavalry."

"That's a considerable number of men, but were the legions not involved?" asked Yan.

"The function of the legions was to fight in the open on battlefields in offensive campaigns and not as immobile defensive units sitting on their backsides in forts. Because they also had considerable expertise in the construction of roads, bridges, aqueducts, forts, ditches, etc., the II Augusta, XX Valeria Victrix and VI Victrix, which had replaced the IX Hispana, were all involved in the actual building of Hadrian's Wall and its forts."

"The identification of the auxiliary troops manning the forts is presumably well documented?" asked Tan.

Windy sighed. "I wish they were. There probably were masses of records, but perhaps only five to ten per cent have survived!"

"So, how is it possible to know which auxiliary units manned where and when?"

"I'm afraid the major source of information comes from inscriptions on altars, tombstones and dedicatory plaques found – usually dug up – during excavations of forts and the cemeteries in nearby settlements, or *vici*."

"Another point", interjected Yan, "is why there were so many cavalry involved? You can't sit a horseman on a wall to fight the enemy!"

"Actually, the original plan was for three massive cavalry forts on the wall, each one strategically sited and containing around 600 cavalry. One, the largest of all of the forts – nine acres in size and containing 1,000 cavalry – was on the western end of the wall at Stanwix (Uxelodunum or Petriana), just over the Eden from Carlisle. Another was roughly in the centre at Chesters (Cilurnum), and the third was on the eastern end at Benwell (Condercum).

"Cavalry, by its very nature, is a mobile force, used to search out the enemy and to determine both its strength and its intentions. Once all of these facts are known, it can be used pre-emptively as a long-range striking force; employed to attack the flanks or rear of an enemy or to mop up retreating or routed foes. On the wall cavalry was employed exactly as outlined, and not parked individually like scarecrows all along its walkway. Good thinking, Batman!"

All three were by now thoroughly banjaxed and suffering from TMI (too much information), so they broke off for refreshments, including a massive kedgeree topped with lobsters – over which the odd questions and answers criss-crossed the refectory table, which sagged ever so slightly under the weight of piles of other comestibles and bottles of red, white and rosé wines.

The main question about the wall was whether it was always so fully manned. The answer was basically yes, apart from times when the Antonine Wall drew men away north to defend that white elephant; when the empire needed troops to defend it against external threats in distant provinces; when usurping governors of Britannia withdrew troops to vie for the imperial throne; when internal revolts and invasions had whittled down the forces in Britannia; and, of course, near the end of the empire, around AD 400, when troops, both legionary and auxiliary, were being withdrawn from Britannia never to return.

The discussions resumed in mid-afternoon after Windy's post-prandial snooze. The boys, although interested in the Roman occupation of the county, wanted to know a bit more about the reaction of the Carvetii and the Setanti to living under both the Eagle and the thumb of the senate and people of Rome.

"Well, I'm sure they didn't like it – especially the Carvetii, whose land was divided in two by Hadrian's Wall. From time to time they revolted, joining uprisings usually instigated by their big brothers, the Brigantes. There is also more than a suspicion that they took part in the Great Conspiracy – a massive multi-pronged and co-ordinated series of external attacks in AD 367–368. Picts and Celts from north of the wall bribed one or more forts to let them through, while at the same time there were seaborne invasions of the north-west coast of Britannia by Irish Celts and penetrating coastal raids in Northern Gaul and Kent by Frisians and Saxons. Simultaneously, there were opportunistic rebellions by disloyal auxiliaries, mostly in the north of Britannia."

"Apart from these overt acts, what was the general attitude of the majority of the Celts?"

"In the southern part of the province of Britannia there were many more and larger towns, and Pax Romana meant prosperity, better housing, gladiatorial games, public baths, better food, wine and generally a more luxurious lifestyle. All these things were very alluring and attractive to the native Southern Celts.

"In the North, there were fewer towns and most people lived, as they always had done, in small family units in farming communities and villages. They traded and bartered with the military and sometimes moved into the *vici* (civilian settlements around the forts). They even struck up relations with the retired soldiers, but on the whole, apart from a few merchants and collaborators, most of the Northern Celts probably kept their heads down for most of the time and waited patiently for the

Romans to leave. When that time finally arrived, the merchant classes and city dwellers vanished into the country, as there were no soldiers left to defend the urban settlements, which were the ideal target for marauding raiders."

It was now late afternoon and Colonel Robinson bade the boys farewell.

"Where are you going next?" he said.

"Not sure," said Yan, "but I think you've given us more than enough to go on with."

"Finding out what happened next will be our next quest," Tan added, "but as to where the answer to that question will come from . . . it might well be on the back of a postcard."

"Which reminds me," said Windy: "I had an invitation yesterday which you might be interested in, though not in terms of your research. There's an exhibition entitled 'The Tablets of Vindolanda'."

"Medical stuff, then – the life and times of dear old Dr Galen?"

"No, these tablets are Roman postcards written in cursive Latin on slivers of wood which have been preserved in acidic soil. They can still be read and open a door into the ordinary world of the soldiers and their families. For example, one was from a mother who had just sent some warm socks up to her son, who had apparently complained to her about the bitter cold in Northumbria. Another was from a Roman matron inviting her friend to a weekend evening dinner party. However, there's been an eye-popping, gobsmacking recent discovery which has got them all in a dither – hence the exhibition. Apparently some really strapping muscular diggers from Down Under – the opal miners of Coober Pedy – unearthed a bombshell: a tablet which revealed not only the recipe, but also the name of the chef who invented that epicurean delight (the Emperor's favourite pudding) *Glaciae Adriani Muri*."

"What does that mean?"

"The ice cream of Adrian Wall – Boom! Boom!"

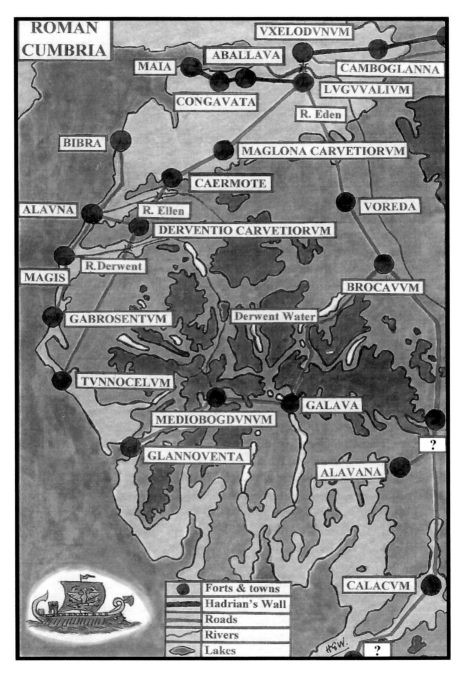

ROMAN
CUMBRIA

VXELODVNVM
ABALLAVA
MAIA
CAMBOGLANNA
CONGAVATA
LVGVVALIVM
R. Eden
BIBRA
MAGLONA CARVETIORVM
CAERMOTE
ALAVNA
R. Ellen
VOREDA
DERVENTIO CARVETIORVM
R.Derwent
MAGIS
BROCAVVM
GABROSENTVM
Derwent Water
TVNNOCELVM
GALAVA
MEDIOBOGDVNVM
?
GLANNOVENTA
ALAVANA

Forts & towns
Hadrian's Wall
Roads
Rivers
Lakes

CALACVM
?

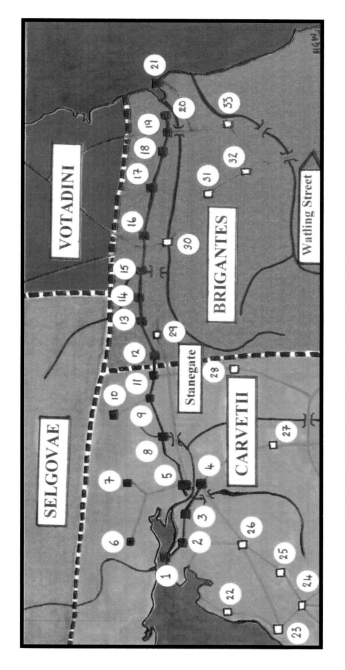

Hadrian's Wall and the Celtic tribes either side of it – *circa* AD 150.

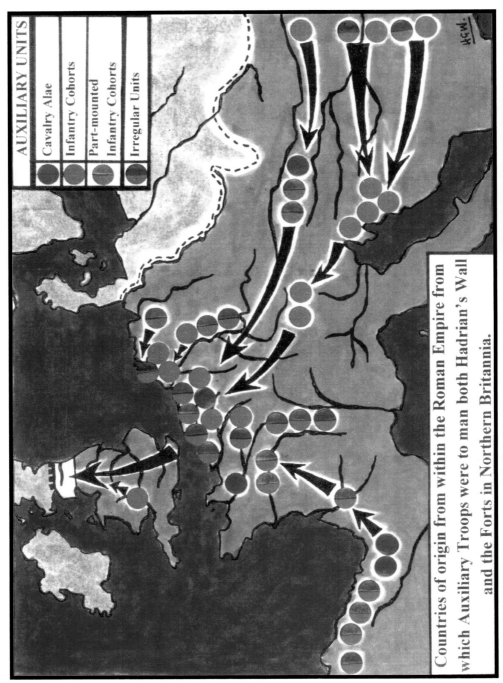

Countries of origin from within the Roman Empire from which Auxiliary Troops were to man both Hadrian's Wall and the Forts in Northern Britannia.

Faraday – The Electric Dog

A doggie peed against a wall.
His name was Faraday.
(In truth a kind of 'setta'.)
But twenty thousand volts
Melted his parts away!
Life could have been betta!

CHAPTER 8 – THE REALLY DIM AGE

"Tan, have you read Emperor Honorius's note dispatched in AD 410 to the 'peoples of Britannia', who had appealed to him for military aid against invading bloodthirsty barbarians?"

"No, what did he say?"

"He was pretty off-hand actually – 'Britannia must look after its own defences.' This sounds remarkably like the title of Douglas Adams's fourth book in the Hitch-hiker's Guide to the Galaxy series – *So Long and Thanks for All the Fish*, which was the message the Dolphins left behind when they left earth just minutes before the Vogon Constructor Fleet destroyed the planet to make way for an Intergalactic Highway."

"Not the best day for Britannia, then – nor, for that matter, earth. So what did the Celts and Romano-Britons do next?"

Yan sat back and attempted to summon a concise answer based on all he had recently read from a pile of uninspiring books, whose chapters generally began with 'Nobody really knows . . .', 'It's not absolutely certain . . .', 'There's no proof written in letters six feet high . . .', 'We didn't find anything much in any of the 1,368 holes we've dug to prove . . .', 'If I could count to twenty with both shoes on and didn't have a pain in my brain, I would tell you the answer . . .', and so on.

"Well," he began, as Yan often did, "the books are, at best, downright vague and their writers seem incapable of arriving at anything definite. However, I have managed to elucidate a few clues taken from five maps, as it happens. The first two indicate the boundaries of the Roman provinces in Britannia in AD 193 and 293. The next one shows the Kingdom of the North, which existed between AD 410 and 450. The last two outline the kingdoms of Northern Britain in AD 450 and 600 – the last one being just before the Anglian invasion of the north-east coast. When viewed in sequence, they demonstrate a pattern which is both logical and makes complete sense."

"Yan, do you think you've cracked it? If so, you really should be very careful. Remember what happened to DNA and don't forget that black-edged advert for a gîte near Eskdale, which Cribb found pinned with industrial staples to the front door – 'Fanciful Amateur Historians Swim with the Fishes in Wast Water.'"

"Point taken; but if we keep this to ourselves for the moment, we should be safe enough."

"Now, as I was saying, Map 1 shows Emperor Septimius Severus's division of the province of Britannia in AD 193 into two parts – Britannia Inferior in the north, with its capital in York, and Britannia Superior in the south, with its capital in London. What is significant about the northern province is that it almost exactly mirrors the region of the earlier Brigantian confederacy. The partitioning of Britannia was the result of a rebellion by the army commander, Decimus Clodius Albinus, and it was hoped that reducing the area over which a general had command – and hence the number of troops at his disposal – would reduce the likelihood of future rebellions."

"Did it work?" asked Tan.

"Not really. Between AD 193 and 296, when Emperor Diocletian decided to divide Britannia yet again, this time into four provinces or dioceses, there had been four rebellions by governors and military commanders."

"Not such a good plan, then?"

"No, but for our purposes this quartering of Britannia, as seen in Map 2, is quite revealing, as the most northerly subdivision, Britannia Secunda, yet again exactly the mirrors the lands of the Brigantian confederacy and – to top it all – its capital was also in York. And before you ask, the division of Britannia into four parts didn't work either as between AD 296 and 407 there were another seven rebellions."

"What does the third map show?"

"This one shows the Kingdom of the North – the first kingdom in the post-Roman period, which lasted from AD 410 to 450. Its boundaries didn't just mirror those of the Brigantian confederacy, they also mirrored those of Britannia Inferior and Britannia Secunda. Equally, it cannot have been a coincidence that its administrative capital was also in the old Roman city of Eboracum, or York."

"Meaning?"

"Firstly, I think it shows more than just a simple pragmatism within the imperial civil service to retain the same boundaries and capital for the two northernmost provinces – basically, because that was the most efficient way to govern the peoples of the North. Secondly, it also suggests that the social cohesion of the Celtic tribes of the old Brigantian confederacy had withstood nearly 400 years of Roman occupation. Proof of that hypothesis is the ease and the rapidity with which the fairly stable and governable region – the Kingdom of the North – came into existence."

"Makes sense!"

"Also, a detailed examination of the last two maps shows a process based on old tribal rather than regional boundaries in the creation of the Kingdom of Rheged. That we will look at later, but at present we should concentrate on the immediate post-Roman period."

What was apparent about the current phase of their research was that the Hardwick boys were not just making better use of Tully Mowze's library, but that they were actually beginning to work as a team. It was also noticeable that there were no more postcards, apart from the one Cribb Swaledale had pinned to the noticeboard with a note asking if Faraday's Wall was one and the same as Hadrian's.

"Well, Tan, what have you learned?"

"Clearly, when the legions left there were many opportunistic raiders, mostly from north of Hadrian's Wall, waiting in the wings to pounce on lands bereft of soldiers. However, in my opinion the North wasn't really that defenceless. The old warrior ethos had not mellowed through soft living, as most of the population had not experienced the relatively comfortable life in towns. Equally, there were plenty of auxiliaries who had retired locally and who had lost neither their military skills nor the ability to teach their sons or neighbours the art of war.

"The peoples in Cumbria and those to the east of the Pennines withstood the initial raids and slowly began to restore a degree of social cohesion and military co-operation, which had once existed in the old tribal areas.

"Sooner or later, a leader was bound to emerge, and one by the name of Coel Hen did around AD 410. He's been referred to as 'the last Roman governor of the North', but that is as valid as his connection with Old King Cole in the early eighteenth-century nursey rhyme. His name, Coel Hen, did actually mean Old Cole, but otherwise little is known of him."

"Are we getting into the Dark Ages?"

"No," replied Tan, "it's just another 40-watt bulb in the alcove, which has just popped again! Actually, the Dark Ages began a bit later on and the term, coined by Francesco Petrarca (Petrarch) – a fourteenth-century poet and scholar – meant that stage in European history when the light of knowledge, fine art, literature, philosophy, law and all the other hallmarks of civilised society was extinguished after the fall of the Roman Empire. The term, at a stretch, has been used for the period between the sixth and fourteenth centuries, but it might just as easily include the century before that – which I am beginning to think of as the Really Dim Age."

"So you're not getting very far, then, Tan?"

"It's a bit of a struggle. . . ."

At which point, in an attempt to pour oil on troubled water, Chibb Swaledale and the Wiggonby Male Voice Choir entered the library, each carrying a battery-operated 40-watt bulb, and sang in complete unison 'Nobody Really Knows', the touching anthem of the Historical Hogwash Society.

"Thank you, men," said Tan, wiping a tear from his cheek. "Well, we actually do know just a little more about Coel Hen, who ruled his kingdom from York and was succeeded by his son, St Ceneu ap Coel."

(Keen scholars of Brythonic Celtic will have noticed the word 'ap', meaning 'son of', which is a telltale clue that this account comes from Welsh Brythonic Celtic sources.)

"Any information relating to Cumbria?"

"Yes, Mor ap Ceneu, 'the Chief of Dragons', succeeded his father in AD 450 and split the kingdom into two – roughly down the Pennine chain. The western half became Rheged and the eastern Ebauc. Rheged consisted of the old tribal lands of the Carvetii, Setanti and the south-western Brigantes, whereas Ebauc had connections with the Brigantes and Parisi."

"Now I see what you were getting at before – these new kingdoms were forming within old tribal boundaries," said Yan with an inkling of insight, "but the map shows Ebauc as being much smaller than you have suggested."

"Actually, the map although dated circa AD 450 is really a little later – perhaps after AD 455, just after the death of the Chief of Dragons, when his kingdom was further divided into Bryneich (the future Bernicia), Old Ebauc and Dewyr (later called Deira)."

"This is getting a little complicated."

"Just hold on to your seat for a second. The first two kings of Rheged were called 'the Unforgettable Ones' – Gwrwst Lledlwm and Meirchon Gul ap Gwrwst. And on the latter's death in AD 535 Rheged was divided into two – North and South Rheged, the former being basically Cumbria."

Tan stopped to take in a deep breath before pressing the intercom button.

"Mr Chibb, I wonder if you could drop what you're doing and kindly help me? Mr Yan has lost the will to live and is banging his head against the stone floor, which I fear will crack unless we do something."

While Yan was convalescing in the old Blencathra TB Sanatorium, Tan went in to see his father and reveal the rest of his research.

Tethra Hardwick almost immediately blurted out, "And before you start, I don't want to hear any of that ap stuff."

"Fair enough – the first King of Northern Rheged was Urien Rheged, the eldest son of Meirchon Gul— Sorry. His capital was in old Luguvalium (Carlisle), from which in AD 550 he launched an invasion of Galwyddel – sorry, the future Galloway. The rest of the history of Rheged is a bit of a mystery, as not a lot is known about it despite about 6,594 holes being dug by archaeologists across Cumbria and South-Western Scotland."

"Son, I thought you were going to sort all this out?"

"You can't make bricks without straw, Fatha! But I can tell you that Rheged became a subkingdom of Northumbria around AD 640 on the death of the last remaining relative of Urien Rheged – his great-granddaughter Princess Reimmelth, who had married Prince Oswy or Oswiu, of Northumbria two years earlier."

Two days later a plain postcard arrived on which were written some detailed instructions, of which the gist was 'The Three Sisters Ash Tree Tea Rooms, Inglewood . . . even you two can't miss them! Be there tomorrow afternoon and don't be late. Blokey.'

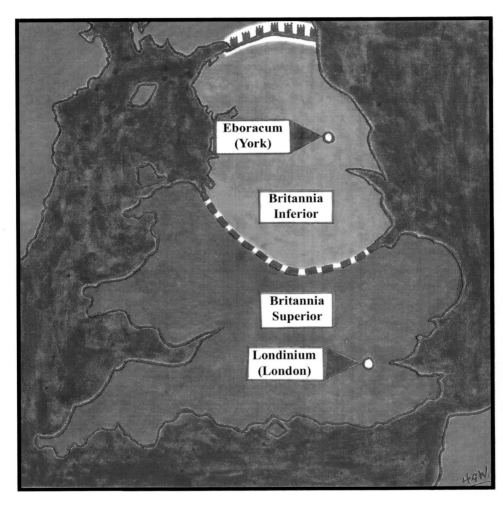

Emperor Septimius Severus's division of the province of Britannia into Britannia Superior and Inferior following the unsuccessful rebellion of Britannia's military commander, Decimus Clodius Albinus, in April AD 193.

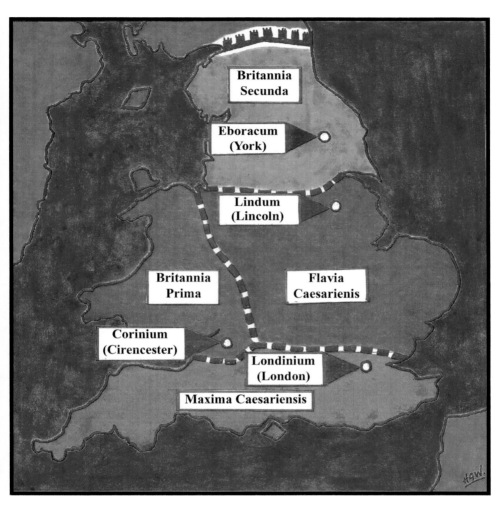

Emperor Diocletian's further division of the provinces of Britannia in AD 296 into four dioceses/provinces – Britannia Secunda, Flavia Caesariensis, Britannia Prima and Maxima Caesariensis (aka Britannia Maxima or Britannia Caesariensis) – following the failed usurpation of the Western Roman Empire by Allectus in AD 293.

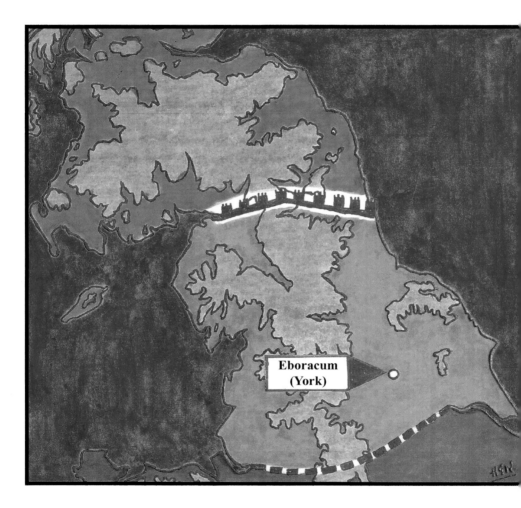

The post-Roman Kingdom of the North, ruled initially be Coel Hen, and then by his son and grandson – St Ceneu ap Coel and Mor ap Ceneu, 'Chief of Dragons' – from AD 410 to 450.

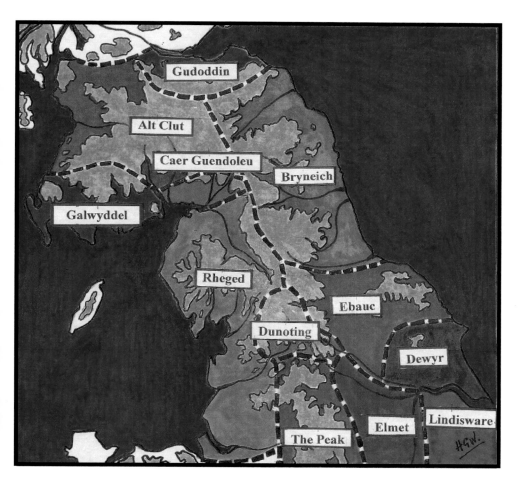

Britain just before the Anglian conquest of the Brythonic-speaking Celtic kingdoms of Northern Britain (circa AD 450).

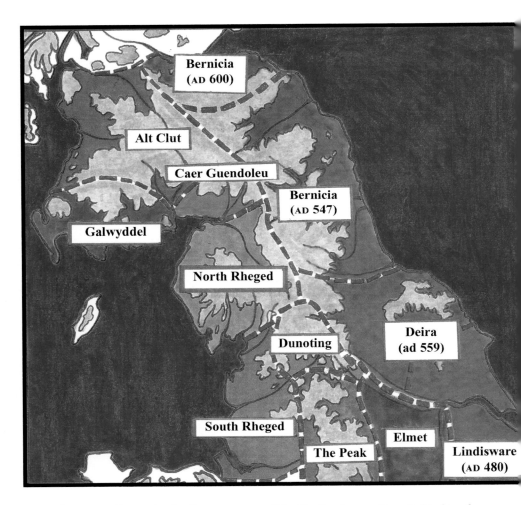

Britain well into the Anglian conquest of the Brythonic-speaking Celtic kingdoms along the north-east coast (circa AD 600). (The dates in brackets indicate the approximate years of these takeovers.)

Blokey's latest disguise and persona: Lev N. Tallstory.

CHAPTER 9 – ANGRBODA'S SANDWICH

Inglewood used to be a massive royal forest stretching almost from Carlisle to Penrith and, according to Andrew of Wyntoun, a Scottish poet and canon of St Andrews in the late fourteenth century, it was home to a few well-known outlaws:

> Lytil Jhon and Robyne Hude
> Wayth-men ware commendyd gude
> In Yngil-wode and Barnysdale
> Thai oysyd all this tyme thare trawale.

Now it's little more than a few scattered patches of woodland in a sea of rich arable and dairy farmland.

Tan picked up his brother from Blencathra the following morning and without much ado the pair headed for Penrith, where they took the old A6 and gunned the Austin 7 northward towards Carlisle. Finding the turn-off to Lazonby, around seven miles up the road and just south of Thiefside Cottages, proved difficult, as a freak summer mist had rolled westward over the countryside from the Eden Valley.

"The Three Sisters Ash Tree Tea Rooms are a mile down this road. They're on the right and at the foot of Bleabury Hill in a clearing next to a very large ash tree," Tan informed his brother, who, despite the swathe of bandages round his head, was his old self.

"What's an ash tree look like, then?" was the reply.

"Easy-peasy – just like that enormous one next to Blokey over there."

"You've changed your name, and your appearance a little, Blokey, but not your clothes," Yan could not resist saying.

"Got to keep ahead of Archaeologists Anonymous – not that they really bother me."

The trio went inside and everything had already been set out – apart from a fresh pot of tea. None of the makings of a Devon cream tea were on the table, but instead there was a loaf of freshly baked bread, some butter and a mouth-watering glass bowl full to the brim with Cumberland rum butter.

"The sisters aren't around today, then," Tan observed.

"No, it's their day off – they're a bit behind with the wool carding, spinning and cutting, so I offered to help out. Couldn't let them get behind with their tally. Our one-eyed boss would not be at all pleased about that."

"In the Land of the Blind . . . Blokey?"

"You don't know the half of it, Tan!"

Tea is a serious business, so it wasn't until it was over and Blokey had brushed the last few crumbs from his maroon silk-embroidered waistcoat that he cleared his throat and said, "You've lost the plot again, boys . . . got too involved with books and have forgotten the broad brushstrokes – too busy bothering about minutia and have completely lost perspective. It's no good harping on and on about Cumbria, Cumbria, Cumbria and Cumbria – you need to look outside the county and take into account the massive upheavals that were affecting the rest of the country . . . so that you can appreciate what subsequently happened within Cumbria when it did. Right?"

"What do we do then – travel miles to see another expert?" both thought and said.

"No – but hang on a moment, there's a raven on the window ledge behind you. No, don't look! He's trying to eavesdrop on our conversation, but I don't think he's heard a word . . . yet. You go out the back door, cross the courtyard and enter the door opposite, while I chase him away."

In Japan they say that life is a dream within a dream, and at that precise moment Yan and Tan were thinking exactly that – or perhaps wondering if the whole afternoon was a daydream in very vivid colours.

The door in question was actually part of the huge ash tree, which towered over the tea rooms. Inside was a spiral staircase which seemed to wind upwards forever. It eventually opened into a fairly homely room, which had a fire and three old women sitting around it, each totally engrossed in the their woolly handiwork. They whispered to each other in a tongue which neither of the boys understood. Then, as if a spell had been broken, they turned round and glared at the boys with eyes which seemed to measure their every dimension.

Then Blokey sidled in and the old women smiled, turned away and continued with their work,

"It's safe now," he said. "We can talk, but not in here – there's another room behind the arras."

The other room was smaller and had only a skylight and three chairs.

"What's this all about?" the boys enquired.

"Some things should remain secret."

"Why?"

"I can't say – not directly – but I can tell you a little by way of the story of 'Snorty' Snorri Sturluson, who came to a sticky end and not because he liked the white powder, which he did by the bucketful. Snorty was born in Iceland, or Arslend in the local tongue, around AD 1179, and became the island's most famous poet, historian and politician. The latter trade is said to have been the cause of his assassination in 1241 on the orders of King Haakon IV of Norway, but that is a total misleading fabrication. Snorty, you see, had broken two rules – he had revealed too many secrets and he had made a lot of his stories up, which would not have mattered that much because that's what most historians do, or at least did in those days. No, where he had made his biggest mistake was in the choice of what and whom he wrote about."

"Which was?" asked the boys, who were both leaning forward lest they should miss a single word.

"He wrote about the gods of Scandinavia, who, although they loved notoriety and tall tales told about them, also liked to keep a few secrets. Now, Snorty was a widely read man and liked to pad his tales out with bits taken from one country or another, from one religion or another or about one god or another. His greatest work, *The Prose Edda*, was a patchwork of tales, fables and legends from Iceland, through Greece and to the Middle East. Naturally, he swore they were all true accounts of life and death in Asgard, Middlegard and Niflheim . . . but they weren't. The long and the short of it was that an unnamed individual was sent by a group of entities, who shall remain nameless, to deal with Snorty, who ended up as the filling in a sandwich eaten by Angrboda, the giantess."

"Nasty!"

"What I am trying to convey to you is that sometimes some secrets – and it isn't always easy to tell which ones – should never be told; and if they are, the consequences can be . . . sticky. Now, the part of your story which you really cannot omit is related to the Scandinavian invasions of Britain. I am prepared to tell you as much as I know, but in stages so that I don't overstep the mark."

Blokey looked up at the skylight, as he thought he had heard a faint tapping. Reassured that he had not, he began Part 1.

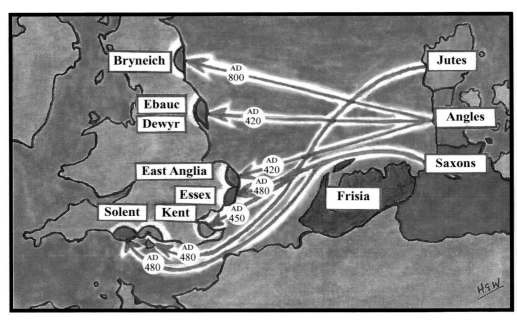

The initial arrival of the Laeti or mercenary warrior bands of Jutes, Angles and Saxons on the east and south coasts of Britain from AD 420 to 500.

CHAPTER 10 – A COLD WIND FROM ACROSS THE NORTH SEA

"Yan," said Blokey, "in your enthusiasm to explain everything, your map theories has caused you to rush through the fifth and sixth centuries, leaving out some important undercurrents and events. So, let's pause for a while and consider the way the wind was blowing."

Then, turning to Tan, Blokey winked and said reassuringly, "And there won't be any more of that ap stuff either. Now, as you pointed out, by AD 450 most things in the garden which the Romans had left behind were doing quite well. The Brythonic-speaking Celts – and please let's not call them Britons, as it makes them sound like lead toy soldiers – had sorted out the initial external threats, patched up most of the internal squabbles and created a number of stable, viable and increasingly prosperous small kingdoms. And, lest there be any doubt, the Celtic kingdoms in Britain extended from the English Channel all the way right up to a line which ran between the Firths of Clyde and Forth. Of these most northerly fiefdoms the most important was Alt Clut, or Clud, which meant 'the valley of the Clyde'. It would become Strathclyde and extend from Dumbarton Rock on the north bank of the Clyde Estuary in a north–south direction – fifty or so miles wide – all the way down to Penrith. That kingdom would play an important role in Cumbria's history."

"Strathclyde was Scottish, right?" asked Tan in a throwaway question.

"No," replied Blokey, "even when it was absorbed through the subterfuge of King Constantine I of Scotland, aka Causantin mac Cinaeda of Pictland, in AD 870 into Alba, the 'fledgling Scotland', it was still a Brythonic-speaking relatively independent Celtic kingdom within which the peoples of Northern Cumbria had asked to be incorporated."

"Now, that is an eye-opener which might upset a few modern politicians. . . . I can't wait to hear the full story," said Tan with a smile.

"For that you'll have to be patient; but for now, let's look at the kingdoms a little to the south. In AD 450 Cumbria and Lancashire constituted the original kingdom of Rheged. The central Pennine region was divided into two kingdoms – Dunoting and The Peak from which the modern name Peak District is derived. In the east was Bryneich, which extended from modern Lothian right down to the Tees. Below that were the remnants of Ebauc and Dewyr. However, nothing ever stays the same, and change is about the only thing that is truly inevitable."

"So what was the factor which altered the status quo?"

"A mixture of laziness, neglect, complacency and mismanagement!"

"Ah," sighed Tan, "politicians!"

"For many years sea raiders from Pictland and the continent had plagued the coastal regions of Britain from the Tyne to the Solent, but the rulers of these regions had steadfastly refused to tackle the problem directly. They preferred the easier option of employing hired help – or Laeti as the Romans used to call such barbarian mercenary warriors. The consequence of hiring Jutes, Angles, Saxons and, to a much lesser extent, Frisians was that the 'barbarians' did not want to go home after being paid for their services. The Celtic kings, again somewhat short-sightedly, gave the mercenary warrior bands small land grants for semi-permanent settlements, rather than recall them later from abroad, when the need arose.

"Between AD 420 and 500 permission for at least seven major settlement sites was granted and they insidiously increased in size due to the appearance of other (uninvited) Danes along with their families. Additionally, the 'guests' became troublesome and difficult to control. Being more skilled and practised in the arts of war than the Celts, these Anglo-Saxons gradually took by force more and more land. Eventually, most of Celtic kingdoms – with the exception of Cumbria, Cornwall and Wales – were in their hands.

"That is the shorthand version of the first Scandinavian takeover of Britain. Modern historians do not believe it took the form of massive and repeated waves of ethnic cleansing by Anglo-Saxons. There obviously was a fair amount of armed conflict, but the takeover was probably more like a change of management – the decapitation of a number of Celtic snakes, on to which were grafted Anglo-Saxon leader's heads – rather that wholesale bloodshed.

"By AD 560 Bryneich had become the Anglian Kingdom of Bernicia, which, after the conquest of modern Lothian, extended its borders from the Firth of Forth to the River Tees. Ebauc and Dewyr also changed hands and name – they were now the Anglian Kingdom of Deira.

"Meanwhile, sitting on the sidelines, the peoples of Northern Rheged – the future Cumbria – kept their heads down, while they should really have been more attentive to what was happening in the lands north of the River Humber.

Between AD 604 and 641 Bernicia and Deira had united three times to form Northumbria – and then had thrice reverted back to its constituent kingdoms. In AD 655 cometh the man, in the form of Oswiu, the son of Aethelfrith of Bernicia, who had in AD 604 ousted King Edwin of Deira, who had brought about the first unification. Oswiu had won the Battle of Winwaed, during which King Penda of Mercia had been killed and the last remaining thorn in Oswiu's side – his nephew King Oethelwald of Deira – had, after deserting King Penda, lost both the respect of everyone and the last chance to become King of Northumbria.

"Don't look so worried, Tan. I've finished the gobbledygook."

"Now, where was I? Yes, Oswiu, it will be recalled, was the man who in AD 638 married the last of the royal line of Urien Rheged – his great-granddaughter Princess Reimmelth, who subsequently died two years later in AD 640. It was from this point in time that Northern Rheged began to become absorbed into the culture of its neighbour. Anglo-Saxon, which some still persist in referring to as Old English, gradually became the dominant language of the county, as more and more Northumbrian Angles took over key posts and important estates. These *yarls* were now the governing class.

"To appreciate the changeover, it is quite enlightening to compare Librarian Potts's Maps 2 and 3 – the Brythonic Celtic and Northumbrian Anglian place-names maps. For the sake of simplicity, he has also used the term 'Anglo-Saxon names', although the Saxons were not in evidence in the North for many years.

"Sixteen of today's villages and towns still retain their Anglo-Saxon names, although they are – inexplicably – situated in the coastal regions of the county. This is odd because the movement into Cumbria by the newcomers was from east to west – along the Tyne–Eden axis or through the Stainmore Gap. However, as noted earlier, toponymy only implies the presence of an ethnic group at a particular site and not migration patterns.

"Although there don't appear to have been any examples of large-scale conflict, it seems unlikely that the changes were accepted entirely with good grace. In fact, around about this time – circa AD 650 – the northern part of Old North Rheged – or Cumberland, as it would become in the twelfth century – along with what is now called Dumfriesshire, the small Celtic Kingdom of Caer Guendoleu, appealed to the Brythonic-speaking Celtic King of Alt Clut in the north to be incorporated into his lands. These three kingdoms then became known as Strathclyde."

"Well I never!" said Tan. "That's another turn-up for the books. I spent hours and hours trying to make sense of the mysteries of mystical Rheged, reading account after account of hundreds of holes being dug all over the place and . . . finding what? Broken pots and unanswered questions!"

"Well done, Blokey," chimed in Yan.

"We are now well and truly into the Dark Ages, but, paradoxically, for the first time there is a lot of historical material to peruse and, although some is not that accurate, having been written a few hundred years later. Between the sixth and eighth centuries the saints Gildas and Bede were busy writing histories – followed by a Welsh monk, Nennius, and two Welsh poets, Taliesin and Aneurin.

"It has to be said that the most readable of all the histories written at this time are the Anglo-Saxon Chronicles, of which there are nine known versions (all being compiled between the ninth and eleventh centuries). Finally, we must not forget the works of William of Malmesbury and Geoffrey of Monmouth.

"Now, unless you like submerging yourselves in the minutia and trivia of the past – which I do not – the best that can be said of the next 200 years is, in my opinion, that really nothing much happened in either the county or country and then it did with a vengeance . . . in the form of Ragnar Lothbrok, his sons and their business colleagues."

"Ragnar the Viking!" both Hardwicks cried out in unison.

"Close . . . but I have to tell you that there were no such things as Vikings. You could say, for example, that Eric Bloodaxe went 'a-viking' – that is, raiding, pillaging and the rest – possibly during a time when he was outside the law for placing his axe in the head of his close neighbour Bjorn-No-Mates, but you cannot call Eric a Viking. The word 'Viking' originated from an Old West Norse name for an inlet or creek – *vik* – and the coastline to the south of Olso, being indented by so many of these features, became known as Vikin, or Viken. An inhabitant of Vikin was known as a Vikingar, of which the plural was Vikingr."

"We stand corrected."

"But as for Ragnar Lothbrok, or Lodrok . . ." Blokey stopped in mid sentence, looked up and gazed directly into the eyes of a large black raven and mumbled something inaudible. "Got to go!" And with that Blokey left abruptly.

"What was all that about?" said Tan.

"I think someone or something just walked over his grave!"

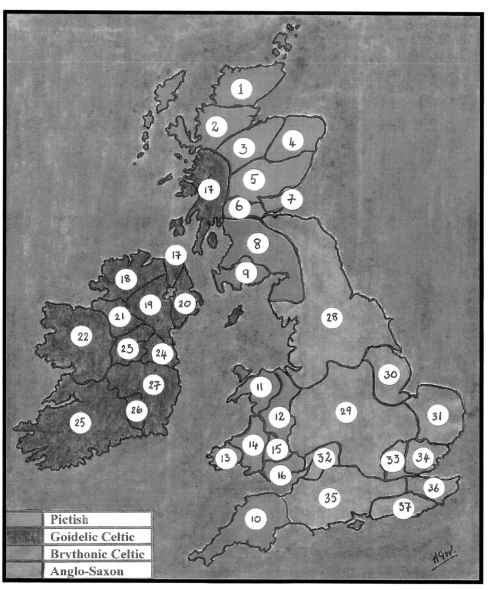

Anglo-Saxon Britain – circa AD 700 – and the different languages spoken across the kingdoms.

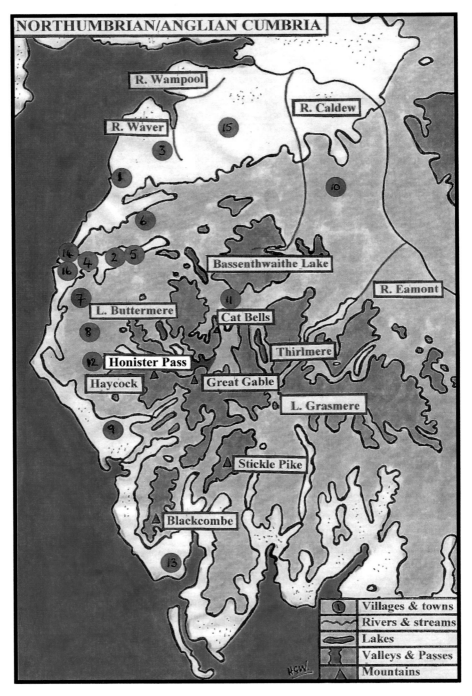

NORTHUMBRIAN/ANGLIAN CUMBRIA

R. Wampool

R. Caldew

R. Waver

15

3

1

10

6

14

2 5

4

16

Bassenthwaithe Lake

7

R. Eamont

L. Buttermere

11

8

Cat Bells

Thirlmere

12 Honister Pass

Haycock

Great Gable

L. Grasmere

9

Stickle Pike

Blackcombe

13

	Villages & towns
	Rivers & streams
	Lakes
	Valleys & Passes
	Mountains

H.C.W.

The Lost Word of Ragnar 'Hairy Breeches' Lothbrok
(A Poetry Competition)

My ingrowing toenail is a curse to me
And gives me hell from one to three,
But now I've written this ode of woe
I've decided to chop off my . . . toe!

CHAPTER 11 – LIFE IN THE FASLANE WITH IVAR THE BONELESS AND OLAF THE WHITE

"I have the distinct impression that there are worse things in life than Archaeologists Anonymous and the Historical Hogwash Society," said Tethra Hardwick on hearing about his sons' most recent meeting with Blokey Bill. "And the meeting took place in The Three Sisters Ash Tree Tea Rooms near Thiefside Cottages . . . to the west of Lazonby?"

"It did," concurred Yan.

"And you actually saw the sisters?"

"We did," his brother added.

"That all rings a distant bell down a seldom-used corridor at the back of my mind. Leave it with me for the present. Oh, and before I forget, Chibb gave me this for you. It's a postcard, or rather an entry form for a poetry competition – 'The Lost Word of Ragnar "Hairy Breeches" Lothbrok'."

"Three guesses as to who sent it – but where are we off to now, Fatha?"

"It looks like to the Roman Fort of Mediobogdum, near the top of Hardknott Pass."

Leaving the Austin 7 at the head of the Eskdale Valley, the boys trudged slowly up the 1 in 3 gradient on the single-track road up the Hardknott Pass to the old Roman fort of Mediobogdum. They were overtaken by groups of OAPs practising for the Tour de Lakeland Wheelbarrow Race.

"Want some of these medicinal herbal leaves from Columbia?" one of the eighty-year-olds offered Yan, while nipping along dressed in a one-man-band outfit.

"No, thank you, it might upset my balance. It's not that easy going backwards uphill walking on your hands!"

"Show-off!" shouted a really old chap in a white jersey covered in large red spots. He was pushing a large cast-iron wheelbarrow with one hand, while trying to strangle a large rabid badger with the other.

"Canny old Cumberland bangs 'em all!" cheered on Blokey, whose head had just popped up from behind the fort's wall. "This way, the Hardwicks! It can't have been much fun for the IV Delmatarum Cohort – a 500-strong infantry unit all the way from Dalmatia – and a real shock to the system in the winter at just over 1,000 feet," continued Blokey, who had hunkered down behind the wall to get out of the wind. "The fort actually only saw service for about sixty years and was part of Hadrian's master plan – as a strategically placed outpost guarding the route from Ravenglass Port (Glannoventa) to Ambleside (Galava). It turned out to be surplus to requirement when Emperor Antoninus Pius built a wooden palisaded defence work between the Firths of Clyde and Forth, known as the Antonine Wall. Hardknott Fort was reoccupied in the early 160s, but may not have been fully manned as the locals sacked it in AD 197. After that it never saw service again."

"Well, you didn't drag us up here for a picnic and a few historical anecdotes . . . but could you just hoy over a veggie bhaji?" said Tan.

"No, we're here disguised as sports officials supervising the tour, so you really should be wearing these rosettes and shouting from time to time a few inane but encouraging words through this bullhorn. It's not safe, you know – even up here."

"If you say so, Blokey . . . but, if memory serves, you were in the process of telling us about Ragnar Lothbrok."

"Some say he never existed – and that he is just a legend – but of course he did. Proof, if needed, can be found in the sagas written about him and his sons. Like those of Njal and Eric the Red, these tales are Icelandic in origin, even though Ragnar and his sons were Danish.

Ivar, Ubba and Halfdan, his sons, took part in the second Scandinavian invasion of Britain and fought in the 'Great Heathen Army' of AD 865. If you thought Norse raiders were a rough lot, then think again – the Danes, who started raiding the coastal regions all round Europe in the latter half of the eighth century, were a thousand times worse. Later on, they abandoned scattered land settlements in favour of the wholesale conquest of Anglo-Saxon Britain. In a nutshell, that was the objective of the Great Heathen and Summer Armies."

"How did Cumbria and Strathclyde fare?" was the inevitable question.

"It's a long story, but well worth the telling . . . and it all began with Ragnar, who was a formidable raider in his younger days. In AD 864 he set out on what was to be his last voyage, heading for his old stamping ground – Northumbria. Off that long wild coast in seas the height of

94

mountains his dragon boat was shipwrecked. His luck exhausted, Ragnar fell into the hands of his old adversary King Aella of Northumbria, who deprived him of a warrior's death by throwing him unarmed into a pit of poisonous snakes.

"His sons, Ivar the Boneless, Ubba and Halfdan Ragnarsson, vowed revenge and took it in AD 866, subjecting Aella to 'the blood eagle' – a most painful death, where the ribs are hacked through along both sides of the spine and the flapping blood-covered lungs pulled out though the gaping wounds.

"The trio weren't very nice to King Edmund of East Anglia either. He had unwisely welcomed the Danes on the arrival of the Great Heathen Army, which had sailed up the Great and Little Ouse rivers in AD 865 to Thetford. He had allowed them to overwinter in East Anglia; had provisioned and then supplied them with horses for their campaign in Northumbria – hoping, probably, that he'd seen the last of them. Having butchered Aella and conquered Southern Northumbria, which they renamed the 'Kingdom of York' – placing the puppet king, Egbert I, nominally in charge – the Danes returned to Thetford. Conveniently forgetting their promise not to harm anyone in East Anglia, they martyred King Edmund in the manner in which Emperor Diocletian had unsuccessfully tried to dispatch St Sebastian to his Maker – riddled with arrows.

"In AD 870 Ivar the Boneless received an invitation from a distant relation, a Norseman called Olaf the White, who had become King of Dublin. Ivar travelled up to York and then headed for Dublin. The next stage of his journey was fraught with problems. A long sea voyage round either the north or south of the British Isles – some 1,000 to 1,200 miles in uncertain weather – with a small fleet of ships would have been a daunting prospect even for an experienced Danish raider. In all probability Ivar took a third option – that of sailing up the Ouse, using portage to cross the Pennines over the old Roman roads and navigating down the Ribble, before crossing the Irish Sea.

"Whatever the case, Olaf, homesick for Norway and bored with his uneventful life, was pleased to see Ivar and looked on him as a possible successor. As a means of testing Ivar's suitability, the two embarked on a massive raid – an attack on the capital of Strathclyde on Dumbarton Rock."

"You did hint at this before," said Tan, rubbing his hands in anticipation.

"The fortress on Dumbarton Rock was formidable, but not impregnable, as it had no direct access to flowing fresh water, which came from streams on the mainland. It was just a matter of besieging the fort, cutting off the water supply and waiting for the cistern on the rock to run dry – which it eventually did.

"King Artgal (the son of Dumnagal) surrendered and was offered to the King of Alba, Constantine I (aka Causantin, the son of Cineada of Pictland), provided he paid a ransom. Handing over the Danegeld, for lack of a better name, was no problem, but – shock and consternation – a live Artgal was. Thus Artgal was killed and Constantine set in motion a plan to marry the daughter of his brother Kenneth MacAlpin to the grieving heir of Strathclyde, whose name was Run. Thus, through murder and subterfuge, the Kingdom of Strathclyde became an unwilling subkingdom of Alba.

"What the subjects of Strathclyde, especially those in the former North Rheged, thought of this change in their governance is not known, but can be fairly accurately assumed. Although by degree Strathclyde was becoming part of the emerging and expanding future Scotland, it remained stubbornly independent until AD 1054, and ever willing to cock a snook at the parent kingdom and its kings.

"By AD 874 Mercia, the massive Anglo-Saxon Central Kingdom of Britain – bordered by Celtic Wales in the west; by Anglo-Saxon Wessex in the south; by Danish East Anglia in the east and by the Danish puppet Kingdom of York in the north – was defeated by the combined forces of the Great Heathen and Summer Danish armies, led by Guthrum and Halfdan Ragnarsson. The former, although ruler of East Anglia, had aspirations to conquer Wessex – the land of Alfred the Great – which he very nearly did in AD 878.

"Weighing up his own prospects of finding a kingdom for himself, Halfdan Ragnarsson saw no future in staying with Guthrum and headed north in AD 875. He took control of Jorvic from its second puppet king, Recsige, and made a beeline for the last Anglian stronghold, Bernicia, whose capital was Bamburgh. Unable to defeat the Angles, Halfdan's second choice of a suitable kingdom to take over was Dublin, where his brother King Ivar the Boneless had died of natural causes in AD 873.

"En route to Dublin, Halfdan called in on Carlisle and sacked this southernmost town of Strathclyde – for no other reason than that it was there and in his way. It seems likely his army was transported across the Irish Sea from Maryport – probably on hired vessels owned by friendly Scandinavian merchants. Within two years, despite gaining and losing the thrones of Dublin and Jorvic twice, Halfdan, the son of Ragnar Lothbrok, was dead – defeated by the Irish King Badir at Strangford Lough."

Blokey paused for a while as Yan and Tan digested this Boy's Own story of blood and mayhem.

"All things considered," said Yan, "the two parts of Cumbria got off fairly lightly."

"The northern part remained in Strathclyde for another 150 years, but it wasn't long before the southern part of the old North Rheged, which had been absorbed into Northumbria, became just another region in the Danish Kingdom of York. The Danes entered the county both over the eastern pass on Stainmore and from the south. With their customary flair for blood-and-guts diplomacy, they took what they wanted, when and where the fancy took them.

"Your Mr Potts has not drawn a separate map adorned with Danish place names; but as Northumbrian Anglian and Danish are so similar, perhaps it's impossible to determine which is which."

"So the county was split into two parts . . . and I suppose you're going to say that the wheel of fortune returned to the old timeless cycle of seasons, which the valley and hill farmers had learned to live with for thousands of years," Yan mused. "That is, until the next set of calamities occurred."

"Well, yes and no," Blokey said in response.

"You're a politician!" retorted Tan, holding his sides with uncontrollable laughter.

"Perhaps . . . but for the moment I shall leave you with two terms: The Pie-King of Iceland, and Danelaw." And with that he was gone again.

The Hardwick Boys looked at each other and shrugged. It had all happened so many times before. Then, instinctively, they turned round towards a sound like chalk on a blackboard – a 'Cawww! Cawww! Cawww!' – and glimpsed a fleeting black silhouette flapping over the southern ramparts.

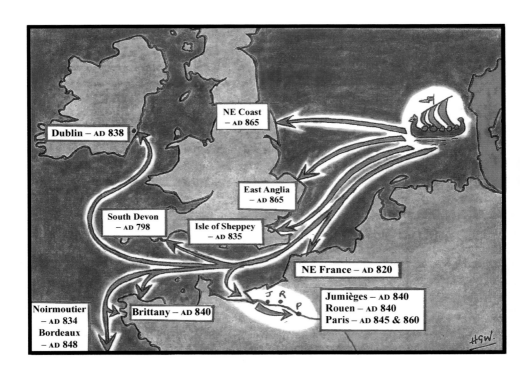

Danish raids – AD 798–865.

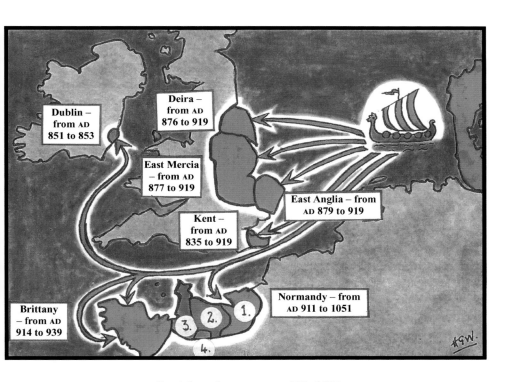

Danish settlements – *AD 835–1035.*

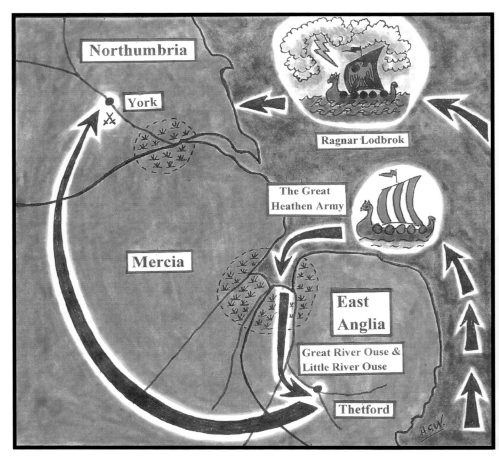

AD 865–866 – the death of Ragnar Lothbrok at the hands of Aella, King of Northumbria, and the subsequent arrival of the Great Heathen Army in East Anglia, where it overwintered in Thetford before heading north to capture Northumbria's capital, York, in November AD 866.

(Great Heathen Army – Map 1.)

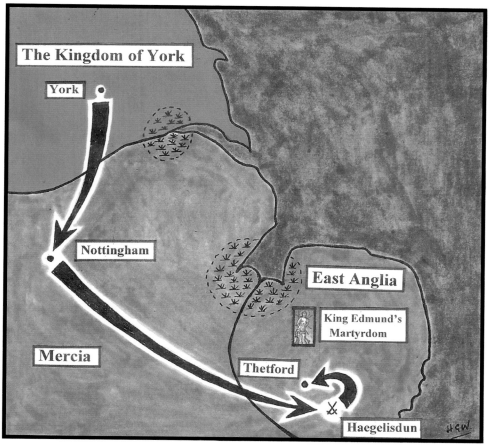

AD 866–869 – after conquering Southern Northumbria, the army invaded Mercia, capturing Nottingham, where it overwintered, before defeating the army of East Anglia and martyring its king, Edmund, in November AD 869.

(Great Heathen Army – Map 2.)

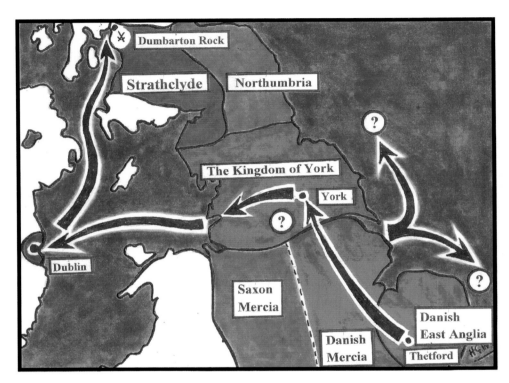

AD 870–871 – Ivar the Boneless left the army and travelled to Dublin, where he and his kinsman King Olaf the White prepared to attack Dumbarton Rock, the capital of Strathclyde, and capture its king, Artgal, in the late autumn of AD 871.

(Great Heathen Army – Map 3.)

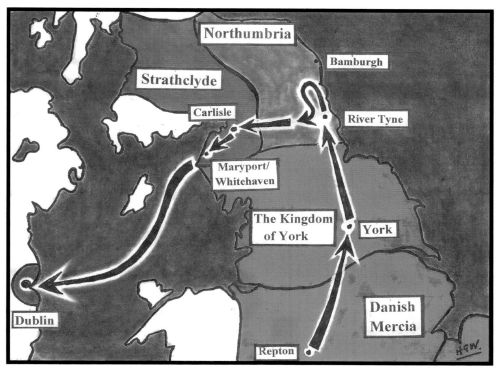

AD 875 – Halfdan Ragnarsson left Repton and, although successful in gaining the throne of Jorvic, failed to defeat the Northumbrian King of Bamburgh. The sacking of Carlisle in Southern Strathclyde occurred while en route to Dublin, where he claimed and won the throne of his brother Ivar the Boneless after killing the incumbent Norse king, Eyestein Olafson, the son of Olaf the White – his kinsman.

(Great Heathen Army – Map 4)

The Pie-King of Iceland.

CHAPTER 12 – POTHOLE NO. 6,459,778 AT MYTH'S END

"If that postcard is from your friend Blokey, then would you be so kind as to give him this package," asked Frank Potts, handing over an A4-sized envelope.

"No problem," replied Tan.

"And Professor Hardwick would like to see you."

"So, you're both off on another trip," said their father. "Where to this time?"

"To a restaurant on the A591 between Thirlmere and Grasmere – just opposite the Lion and the Lamb. It's called, of all things, 'The Pie-King of Iceland'," replied Yan, holding up a postcard.

"Your friend, Blokey, may not be all he appears to be. Just look at this," their father continued, giving Yan a yellowing and faded copy of the *Cumberland News*, dated 14 March 1941.

The top left column on page 3 revealed:

'Glasgow suffers yet another Blitz and stray bombs are dropped randomly on Cumberland by a returning bomber. Three elderly women were believed killed at a tea room on the back road to Lazonby, which was totally destroyed.'

There was an ominous silence as all three exchanged looks of disbelief.

"Be careful, boys," their father warned as he waved them off.

The road from Keswick to Grasmere is more than just scenic – it's stunning. Thirlmere, below Helvellyn, looked like a mirror, reflecting all the greens in nature's palette that sunny morning. There wasn't much traffic, but at the bottom of Dunmail Raise they had to stop at some temporary traffic lights which seemed stuck on red. On the left-hand side of the road was a sign which proclaimed, 'Roadworks: Cumbria County

Council proudly announces the filling in of Pothole No. 6,459,778.' Or was it '779'? – the number was smudged.

"Work in progress . . . maybe they filled in 779 earlier today," Tan observed.

Just then 'Dan, the Shovel Operative Man' came over and apologised for the delay, which apparently was due to a key worker having to make an emergency trip to a local farm to borrow a cup of sugar. The boys got out to stretch their legs and survey the scenery.

"No. 6,459,778 must be a really big hole – there are two large piles of stones, one on either side of the road," Tan observed.

"The one on the right isn't a pile of stones – it's a cairn, and not any old cairn!" retorted Yan. "It's the cairn under which the last King of Cumberland, Dunmail, is said to have been buried."

"Oh," said Tan, mouthing something else, "I wish I'd brought my camera."

Just then the light turned to green and they resumed their journey passing through at least thirty workmen in two lines, cheering and drinking tea.

The Lion and the Lamb is the outline of Helm Crag, as seen from the road below against the western skyline. It appears in silhouette exactly as its name suggests.

The Pie-King of Iceland is, on the other hand, a glorified pub just off the A591 and opposite the crag. For reasons known only to himself, the owner, Harkon Nottomey, only served pies filled with nine-month-matured basking-shark fillets, prepared from a secret recipe of his wife's late grandmother, Sally Monellar. It is for this precise reason that the establishment is usually empty – and why, more importantly, Blokey had chosen it for their meeting.

"Not having the pie, boys? They each come with a strong paper bag, which I suspect has nothing to do with doggy bags."

"No," replied Tan. "I would rather eat my own foot!"

"Which oddly enough is what the cook, John Silver, on the *Hispaniola* in *Treasure Island*," said, as I recall. But enough of this idle banter, and let's get down to business. Danelaw or Danelaugh – (*Danelagen* in Danish) – is a confusing historical term which first saw the light of day on vellum in the Anglo-Saxon Chronicles. It sounds like one thing, but actually means another."

"I knew a politician like that – he was called Duplicitous Dave," said Tan.

"Danelaw is much easier to show you on a map than to explain, and I just happen to have one which I prepared earlier. Basically, the term is used to identify all those Anglo-Saxon lands which the Danes had conquered and where everyone was subject to Danish laws. As you can see, it consisted of the lands of Guthrum in East Anglia, the Danish burghs of the South, Danish Mercia and the Kingdom of York. The term first came into usage after Alfred the Great had defeated Guthrum at the Battle of Edington in Wiltshire in AD 878, after which they both signed the Treaty of Wedmore in Somerset – marking the cessation of Danish expansion and the birth of an aspiration, which the sons and grandsons of Alfred the Great would bring to fruition.

"Alfred's hope was that one day there would be one Anglo-Saxon kingdom for the whole of the country, which would be called Englaland, the land of the Angles, which is somewhat of a misnomer since it would be created by West Saxons and ruled by the Kings of Wessex. For this dream to become reality a sequence of events would have to take place. Firstly, the newly formed lands under Danelaw would have to be dismembered piece by piece. Secondly, the other kingdoms – Anglian Northumbria and Celtic Cornwall – would need to be brought under Anglo-Saxon control. To this end, and for the next fifty years, the Kings of Wessex would work with fervour and zeal."

"You didn't mention Cumbria," Tan interrupted.

"And for two very good reasons: the southern (Northumbrian) part of the county would take fifty years to achieve this, whereas the northern part, which had voluntarily been incorporated into the Kingdom of Strathclyde, would have to suffer a much longer delay – in fact it would not become part of England until AD 1032, and then only on the instigation of a Danish king called Knud."

"I thought you implied that the Danes had been sent packing by then!"

"They had, but they came back briefly yet again!"

"Persistent beggars, weren't they?"

"You have no idea, but you will in a short while."

In the last few minutes dark grey rainclouds had piled up over central Lakeland and the odd clap of thunder echoed distantly round the mountaintops. Then a near-apocalyptic explosion of sound rent the air and a shard of lightning stabbed the earth near Grisedale Tarn, just to the north.

"Oh, and before I forget, Mr Potts asked us to give you this," said Tan as he handed over the envelope.

"That must be his last map – no, there are two, which I shall study in due course – but first we must get from Alfred to Aethelstan, as it were, but without straying too far from the path." Then, taking a deep breath and trying his best not to think too much about nine-month-matured basking sharks, he began:

"Edward the Elder succeeded Alfred in AD 899 as King of Wessex, and, after a pause of a few years, slowly began to convert his father's dreams into reality. By AD 911 London, Oxfordshire and Middlesex were in his hands. In AD 913 Essex became part of Greater Wessex, followed by the rest of East Anglia five years later.

"That same year, AD 918, Mercia was reunited after the capitulation of the nine Danish burghs in the east, and was ruled for a few months by Edward's sister, Aethelflaed – the Lady of Mercia – until her death, when Edward took control of the whole of Mercia.

"On Edward's demise in AD 924 the dismemberment of Danelaw was still incomplete. The succession passed to his son, Aelfweard, but he died at the age of twenty-one years within sixteen days of his father."

"And the death certificate said?" enquired Tan.

"There weren't such things in those days, but if there had been it might have inferred his demise was due to either an hypnopompic state induced by profound horripilations and pandiculations."

"Or just plain murder," interjected Tan.

"The latter suspicion was probably the reason why his half-brother, Aethelstan, who had inherited Mercia, was not recognised by the Witan as the King of Greater Wessex until AD 924," continued Blokey.

"As it happened, it was Aethelstan who was to fit together the last three pieces of marble in the mosaic Alfred had called Englaland. In the year AD 927 the Kingdom of York was his, and shortly after that the Anglian Kingdom of Bernicia/Northumbria submitted to his overlordship. The Brythonic-speaking Kingdom of Cornwall was defeated the same year, but Aethelstan needed more than mere military conquests to support his claim. He needed the recognition of the other major players in the British Isles, and to this end he arranged for two important meetings to take place.

"On 12 July AD 927 Aethelstan met King Constantine II of Scotland at Eamont Bridge near Penrith, just over the southern border of Strathclyde, where the latter accepted Aethelstan as his overlord. Within weeks it was the turn of the Kings of Wales to journey to Hereford to pay homage to Aethelstan, who could now rightfully call himself the first King of England. Indeed on the continent of Europe he was known as the Emperor of Britannia."

"Now, that was a tale and a half! Constantine II of Scotland actually submitted to Aethelstan at Eamont Bridge." Tan smiled and added, "I wish I'd been there!"

"Yes, it must have been quite a show – but nothing lasts and no one lives forever. Aethelstan died at Gloucester on 29 October in AD 939, aged only forty-four, but, more importantly, he died childless. He was succeeded by the sixteen-year-old Edmund, the youngest son of King Edward the Elder by his third wife, Eadgifu of Kent.

"It had never been auspicious to become a king at an early age and, even worse still, as a child. Edmund was on the cusp of manhood and was inexperienced in everything a king should know about and be proficient in. He knew this only too well, as did the ruling elite of Northumbria and the Danish *yarls* in the North.

"More importantly, there was another person, Olaf Guthfrithson, King of Dublin – a man of mixed Norse and Irish ancestry – who would take full advantage of Edmund's and England's weaknesses.

"To cut a long and tortuous story short, Olaf invaded the north of England in late AD 939 – probably making landfall on the Wirral. He travelled to York along the old Roman roads and on his arrival was proclaimed as king of both York and Northumbria. Then, despite an agreement with Edmund at Leicester that same year in which he declared he had all the land he would ever require, Olaf – a man not averse to breaking his word – soon incorporated the five old Danish burghs of East Mercia into his kingdom.

"At this point the fickle finger of fate intervened and Olaf Guthfrithson died in AD 941. His cousins, who succeeded him, were not made from the same mould and were no match for King Edmund I, who by AD 944 had regained all the lands that had been taken from him."

"Does this really have anything to do with our research?" asked Tan, his face grimaced in a suppressed yawn.

"Have patience and all will be revealed" was Blokey's reply.

"King Edmund was nigh on unstoppable in AD 944. His armies marched on through Northumbria and into Strathclyde, where they defeated its forces with consummate ease – probably in reprisal for King Owain I of Strathclyde's support for an earlier invasion of England by Olaf Guthfrithson in AD 937.

Edmund promptly gave Strathclyde back to King Malcolm I of Scotland – both as a gesture of goodwill and in the hope of future military co-operation, should it ever be required, against the Norse Gaels of Orkney,

Shetland and the Western Isles. Then, as a token of Malcolm's good faith, Edmund asked him for assistance – although, in truth, he really didn't need any help – in the pursuit of the fleeing leader of the armies of Strathclyde, – aka Dunmail, the last King of Cumberland."

"We saw his cairn at the bottom of Dunmail Raise this very morning!" cried out Tan in excitement.

"Well, I have to tell you", related Blokey with a degree of reticence, "that not everything in stories told to Cumbrian children is entirely accurate. Firstly, he wasn't called Dunmail. More than likely, his name was Domnal mac Domnal, or possibly Donald MacDonald, or even King Dyfnwall ab Owen II of Strathclyde. And he wasn't the first or even last King of Cumberland. He did actually exist and probably was the King of Strathclyde. Fleeing south with his sons and remnants of his army, he died fighting the combined forces of Edmund and Malcolm. His sons took his crown and scaled the local fells to the east, where they cast it into the black depths of Grisedale Tarn. For their defiance, and to prevent their ever becoming a leader of any future rebellion, they were castrated and blinded."

"Hard times" was all that Yan could muster.

"Legend has it that, one day in the future, should Cumberland be in peril, and a native-born son of the county were to retrieve the golden crown and place it on the cairn at midnight during a full moon, then the dead king would return and disaster would be averted!"

"Shades of King Arthur," Yan said under his breath.

At that moment the door to the kitchen swung open and Bjorn Allhoep, the Swedish chef, burst in, declaring, "The pie is off!"

"Nothing's on the menu now!" chortled Tan.

"No-o-o! The cat ate some pie and died! Ooooh, and there's a telephone call for a Mr Blokey, Loki or whoever you are."

After about an hour, Blokey hadn't returned, so the boys headed back up the A591 and stopped at the bottom of Dunmail Raise to exchange a pleasantry or two with Dan, the Shovel Operative Man, who was just packing up his gear. It was only then that they noticed that both piles of stones had disappeared.

"Dan, what happened to the cairn?" they both shouted.

"It was a very big pothole, and it took a lot of filling!"

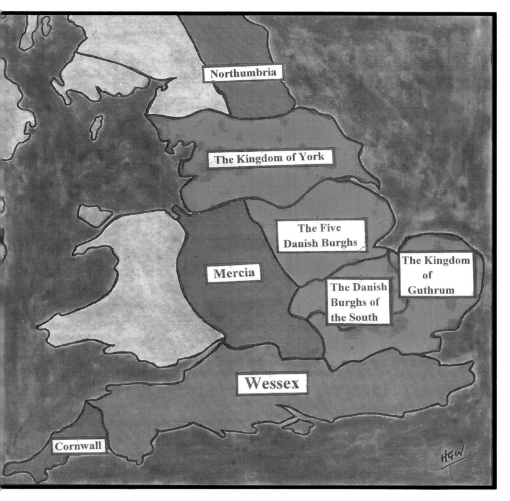

The lands under Danelaw – AD 878.

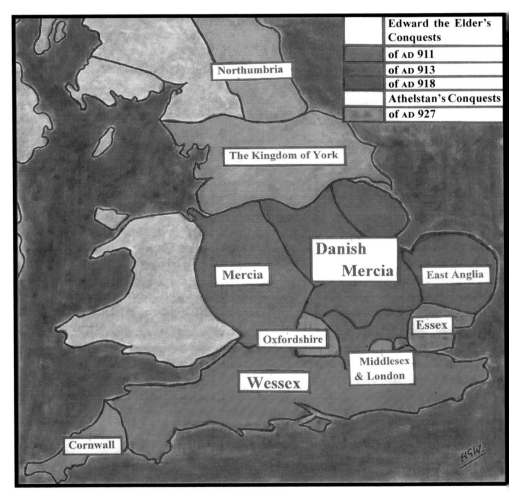

The dismemberment of Danelaw – the conquests of King Edward the Elder of
Wessex and King Aethelstan, the first king of England, between AD 911 and 927.

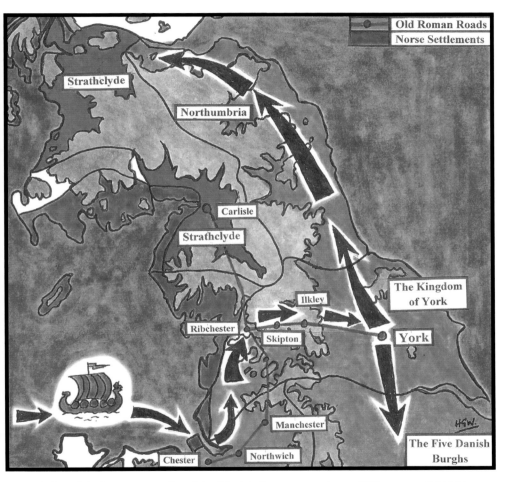

Olaf Guthfrithson's second and (unlike his first attempt in AD 929) successful bid in AD 939 to become the ruler of the Kingdom of York/Jorvic.

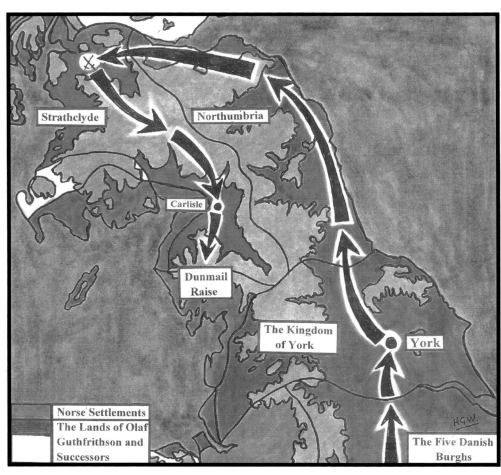

King Edmund I's campaigns in AD 942 and AD 944 to retake the northern Kingdoms of York and Northumbria and the five Danish burghs gained by Olaf Guthfrithson in AD 939, and the subsequent Strathclyde campaign of AD 945.

Speatrie, near Bifrost Bridge and Valhalla.

CHAPTER 13 – NORSE, SOUTH, EAST AND WEST

"How did the meeting go?"

"Well, the dish of the day killed the cook's cat and Blokey disappeared again, Fatha. Other than that, it was uneventful," replied Yan.

"Bad penny – he'll turn up again."

"Well, for the moment we're short on information – the Norse, to be precise," added Tan.

"Perhaps I can help; but first of all, do you like my new picture of Speatrie? I do, but every time I pass it I can't help singing that old sixties jingle on Border TV about 'Quality puff pastry from Aspatria'."

"How did it go, Fatha?"

"Shut up, Tan!"

Professor Hardwick composed himself and then laid out two maps on his desk, which outlined the extent of Norse raids and settlements between AD 750 and 1000.

"As you can see, they were first class seamen and navigators, who must have used their accumulated knowledge of wind and sea, as well as information from merchants, maps, star positions and sun sightings, to guide them to their destinations. They didn't just hug the coasts, but crossed wide stretches of open water. We are only now just beginning to appreciate how really skilled they were. Actually, they used a whole array of instruments and techniques to help them – like weather vanes to show wind direction, 'bearing circles' to give a rough estimation of latitude, 'sun stones' to identify the position of the sun on cloudy or foggy days and 'sun boards' to judge the time of midday."

They discovered many islands in the North Atlantic, but to their amazement – and to ours now – they found monks from either Ireland or Scotland in residence or evidence of their earlier occupation in the form of dwellings and religious artefacts."

"I know," said Yan, "the Norse and Danes had their dragon boats, which were both robust and pliable enough to cope with the open seas, but also, being of shallow draught, they could sail up most rivers. However, what type of vessel did the monks use?"

"Amazingly, in wooden-ribbed small boats covered in cattle skin, called curraghs – goodness knows how many of them perished on their voyages to find unknown lands with pagans just waiting to be converted!"

"We've heard about the Danes with their terrible reputation, but what about the Norse – were they any different?"

Professor Hardwick scratched his head, paused and then hesitantly offered his opinion.

"*Homo sapiens* is violent by nature – always has been – but not all are the same and not all circumstances provoke the same behaviour. Raids are one thing, but setting up settlements is perhaps another. There were bound to have been instances of bloodshed and forceful eviction of native farmers and communities . . . but as to whether the Norse were any different from the Danes, it is not known. They certainly have been tarred with the same brush by monks in their scriptoria, but that is to be expected.

"Evidence of widespread slaughter, when the Norse settled in Cumbria, is absent. It goes without saying that the dead make poor witnesses, but there are always survivors to give first-hand accounts . . . but none have been found.

"With regard to when the Norse settlement of Cumbria occurred, it is generally accepted that there was a gradual influx from the west coast of Scotland and from Northern Ireland – rather than directly from Norway – from about AD 850 to 900 or thereabouts.

"However, the Norse settlers of Dublin, who had evicted the Danes in AD 853, were themselves unceremoniously kicked out of that kingdom in AD 902 by Irish Celts. They sailed west to the Isle of Man and the coast of North-West England – including Cumbria. The numbers were probably large enough to provoke little resistance. This was also at a time when Cumberland was still part of Strathclyde, and Westmorland was part of the Danish Kingdom of York. A completely unified Englaland did not as yet exist, so any armed response would have been localised rather than well organised and centrally based."

Two other maps were taken out and put on display – Mr Frank Potts' maps of Norse Cumbria."

"Did you know, boys," the Professor continued, "that Mr Potts was inspired to produce all of his masterpieces because of the mindless inspiration of an academic whose only other claim to fame was an Olympic bronze medal in the mixed synchronised swimming?"

"Really?"

"No, of course not – he was disqualified, but his theory was accepted by all the other academics for years. He maintained that, because the Danes had come from a flat country, where animal husbandry involved looking after cows and pigs, they preferred to settle on the flat coastal plains and river valleys of Cumbria. The Norse, on the other hand, having come from a mountainous country with long, deep fjords, just like our lakes, and because they were familiar with hill farming and the rearing of sheep, preferred to settle in the centre of the county – the Lake District."

"Amazing really," said Tan, "but what can you expect from monkeys!"

"That is species-ist, but quite correct. Looking at Mr Potts' place-name maps, it seems pretty obvious that the Norse settled absolutely everywhere."

"Also," pointed out Yan, "if you compare these two – and he couldn't get all the information on one – on all of his maps the Norse names far outnumber all the others put together. There are thirty-seven villages and towns, six streams, thirteen tarns and lakes, sixteen valleys and passes and ten hills and mountains. What do you make of that?"

"Well," said Tethra, "there's just so much you can infer from maps like these. Specific ethnic names – Norse, for example – only mean that those people once lived in those villages or near those topographic features. It does not mean that earlier settlers from different ethnic backgrounds had not lived there before the Norse arrived. Perhaps, quite simply, the Norse, in occupying these sites, just renamed them with names of their own liking and in their own tongue. Also, some say that because they formed, in effect, the last major influx of settlers, their place names are just an example of the last man standing choosing the names of the places . . . but then, you've heard all this before."

"However," Tan interjected, "it does not detract from the simple fact that the Norse settlement across the whole of the county was massive and that their influence is still with us. Their place names are what we call things and places today – without knowing what they might originally have meant. Additionally, many words from their language are now part of the dialect and taken for granted."

"I stand corrected. Now, is there anything else you would like to know? And I am not referring to *Ovo bipedus* and the Herdwick sheep coming over with the Norse, which is something too close for comfort."

"No!"

"Well, there should be. There's something which has been nagging at me for some time – something which cannot be ignored."

"Go on."

"Well, I have told you previously that Iceland converted, virtually en masse, to Christianity in AD 999 because they had been told by priests that the end of the world was at hand – i.e. in AD 1000. Yes, well, the missionaries had been prattling on to everyone about that for decades, but without much success as the Scandinavians were confirmed pagans who believed in the old gods and knew their place in the meaning of life, death and Ragnarok. Their concept of reality was that the earth they stood on was flat and the middle layer of three worlds, which were intimately connected by the World Tree – an enormous ash called Yggdrasil. Under that tree three women spun, wove and cut the measured thread of life of each and every man, woman and child born in Middle Earth or Midgard. They were the Norns – Urd (Fate), Skuld (Being) and Verdandi (Necessity) – just like the Fates, or Moirai, to the Greeks, the Parcae to the Romans and the Sudice to the Slavs."

"This is sounding very familiar," said Yan, "and reminds me of Angrboda's sandwich."

"And so it should . . . but there's more! Midgard was where men, elves, dwarves and the frost giants lived – a circular land surrounded by the Poison Sea, in which lived the giant serpent Jormungand – its tail solidly gripped in its own teeth in a massive circle around Midgard.

"The lowest of the three worlds was an eternally dark, cold and evil place called Niflheim, the Realm of the Dead, where Nidhogg, the Corpse Tearer, an ever hungry dragon, ate the dead and chewed at the roots of Yggdrasil. This realm was ruled over by Hel, a monster and the daughter of . . ."

"Of whom?"

"I shall come to that shortly. Now, Asgard was the topmost world and the home of twenty-four gods and goddesses. It was connected to Midgard, beneath it, by Bifrost – the Flaming Rainbow Bridge – which was guarded against intruders by Heimdall.

"Men who have died heroically in battle, weapon in their hand, had a chance of entering Asgard if picked by the Valkyries, warrior maidens who transported them to Valhalla, the home of 'All-Father' Odin, the kings of the gods. Life in Valhalla was basically fighting all day and drinking/womanising all evening and night. Even if they 'died' during these reveries, the next day it began all over again. But this supposedly idyllic warrior existence was not destined to go on forever. It would all end one day . . . as would all of the worlds in the final Battle of Ragnarok.

"A slow build-up of calamities in Midgard – starting with Fimbulvetr, the Winter of Winters – would signal the coming end. Finally, three cockerels would crow – an unnamed soot-red one in the halls of the underworld; a red one, called Fjalar, in the Land of the Giants and golden-combed Gullinkambi on the roof of Valhalla – to summon the armies for the final contest.

"The heroes would file out of Valhalla's 540 doors in contingents of 800 and march with the forty-eight gods to the wide Plain of Vigrid in Asgard to fight the Frost Giants and an assortment of monsters. The result of this battle would basically be the end of everything – but possibly a few might survive, including some of mankind."

"So, what you are saying", said Yan, "is that the Scandinavians believed in a religion which, to put it simply, had as a bottom line that, despite a possible few years of a good time in Valhalla, there really was no hope whatsoever of anything to look forward to in the end."

"That just about sums, it up and was the reason for the warrior culture which sustained them," said Tethra Hardwick. "Very depressing in most respects; but they, on the other hand, didn't think much of Christianity. It had far too many rules and constrictions which their gods did not try to impose on them. Their gods had a touch of humanity about them – in that, in some respects, they were just as flawed as humans and would on occasion visit Midgard in disguise to share in the worldly pleasures of life. They let mankind get on with life . . . and even though there was an inevitability about the final outcome, it was possible on death to avoid the underworld and win a place in Valhalla."

"Well," said Tan, "I suppose it does explain why some of them behaved as they did, but what a miserable way to look on existence."

"True," continued their father, "but this is not a theology or philosophy seminar . . . and what I have been trying to do was to explain your experiences of today in yesterday's terms. You see, of the twenty-four gods, two undoubtedly give me concern. The first was 'All-Father' Odin – the king of the Scandinavian gods – who had sacrificed one eye to be allowed to drink from Mimir's Well, which was entangled in the roots of Yggdrasil. He did this in order to gain wisdom and insight. It was also he, more than most, who frequently roamed Midgard – bent over like an old man, dressed in black and wearing a pointed hat as a ploy to keep an eye (his one eye) on mankind. He also used two large black ravens, called Huginn and Muninn, for the same reason. They flew far and wide across Midgard, only returning to their master when they had important news."

"Where have we heard that before?" the boys replied.

"Where indeed?" murmured their father. "Which brings me round to the second god, the father of Hel and someone you may know of by another name. This god was a trickster, a mischief-maker, a shape-changer and . . ."

"AND WHAT?"

"Enough of this spoon-feeding – it's time you worked out a few things for yourselves, and, truth to tell, I've given you enough clues.

"Ah, here comes your old friend Chibb – and, if I'm not mistaken, he has a postcard which I perused earlier. It's from the Reverend Gunnar Mangison, the locum vicar of St Mary's Church in Gosforth, who as luck would have it – which were his precise words – has information to your advantage."

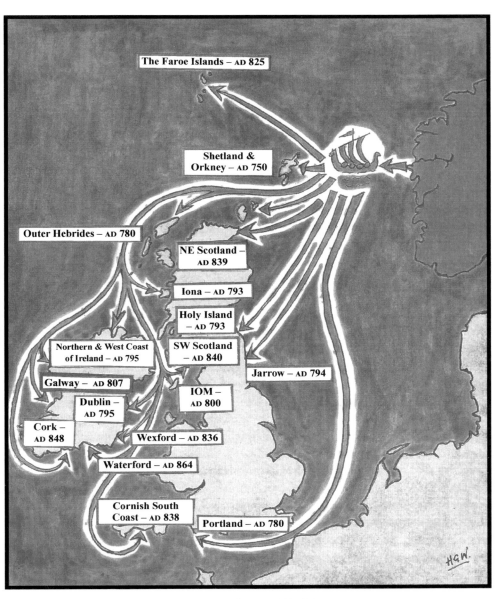

The Faroe Islands – AD 825

Shetland & Orkney – AD 750

Outer Hebrides – AD 780

NE Scotland – AD 839

Iona – AD 793

Holy Island – AD 793

Northern & West Coast of Ireland – AD 795

SW Scotland – AD 840

Jarrow – AD 794

Galway – AD 807

Dublin – AD 795

IOM – AD 800

Cork – AD 848

Wexford – AD 836

Waterford – AD 864

Cornish South Coast – AD 838

Portland – AD 780

Norse Raids – AD 750–864.

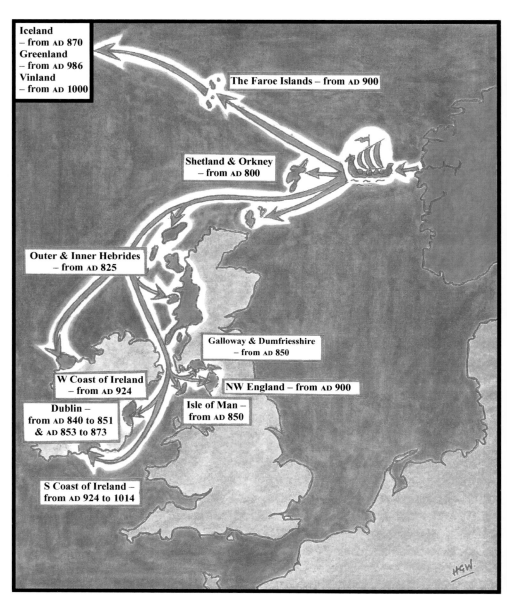

Iceland
– from AD 870
Greenland
– from AD 986
Vinland
– from AD 1000

The Faroe Islands – from AD 900

Shetland & Orkney
– from AD 800

Outer & Inner Hebrides
– from AD 825

Galloway & Dumfriesshire
– from AD 850

W Coast of Ireland
– from AD 924

NW England – from AD 900

Dublin –
from AD 840 to 851
& AD 853 to 873

Isle of Man –
from AD 850

S Coast of Ireland –
from AD 924 to 1014

HGW.

Norse Settlements – AD 800–1014.

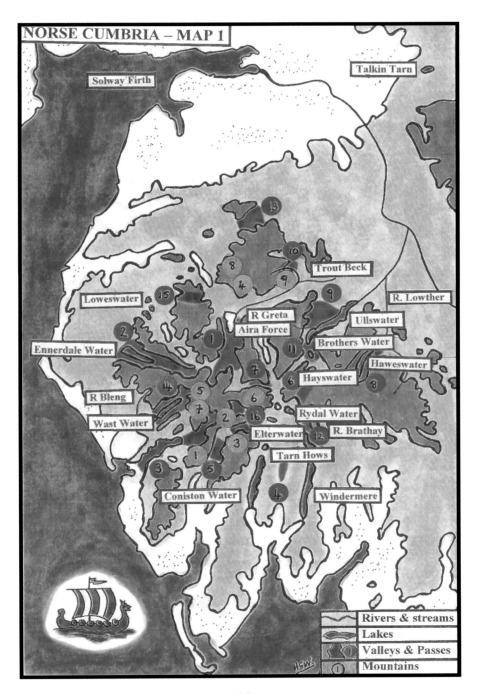

NORSE CUMBRIA – MAP 1

Solway Firth

Talkin Tarn

Trout Beck

R. Lowther

Loweswater

R Greta
Aira Force

Ullswater

Ennerdale Water

Brothers Water

Haweswater

R Bleng

Hayswater

Wast Water

Rydal Water

Elterwater

R. Brathay

Tarn Hows

Coniston Water

Windermere

	Rivers & streams
	Lakes
①	Valleys & Passes
①	Mountains

125

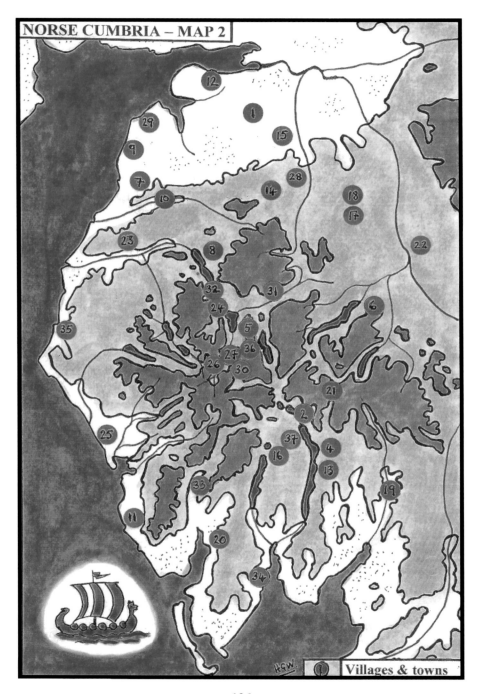

NORSE CUMBRIA – MAP 2

Villages & towns

126

St Columba and St Martin's Cross on Iona.

CHAPTER 14 – A GREAT DANE IN GOSFORTH AND A GAME OF NORSE AND CROSSES

"It's a conundrum and no mistake," said Tan as they were overtaken by an American limousine on the A595 south of Egremont.

"I've heard of a Panjandrum, but never a car called a Conundrum."

"Oh really, Yan – I mean, I can't work out what's in it for us going all the way down to St Mary's at Gosforth to meet this Reverend Gunnar What's-his-name?"

"Perhaps he wants to tell us about U664, which used to be in the churchyard and is now in the British Museum."

"A submarine?"

"No, U664 is a code – the 664th in an alphanumeric coding system used to identify large ancient stones covered in runes," replied Yan. "This one stood in the churchyard of St Mary's for centuries and all but one of its runes were chiselled off by a gravedigger in the last century, who wanted the four-foot-high stone for his own grave. The rune he left was 'Knud', which in Danish is Canute."

"Which was the gravedigger's name?"

"No – it was a Friday afternoon and Bert knocked off early!"

"And the original Knud – was he anyone special?" enquired Tan, half stifling a yawn.

"He was Canute the Great, and the son of Sweyn Fork-Beard. Both invaded England in AD 1013 at the head of a formidable Danish army, causing Aethelred II, the Unready, to flee to France, where he took refuge with his wife's father, Richard I, Duke of Normandy."

"I've heard of Aethelred."

"Who hasn't!" retorted Yan. "But do you know what his Anglo-Saxon name really means?"

"No, but I'm sure you're going to tell me, Oscar Fingal O'Flahertie Wills Wilde!"

"Very funny! It means something like 'well advised' or 'well prepared'."

"A better name would have been Aethelred the Useless. He didn't defend England with an army or a navy, preferring to pay the Danes with Danegeld – some 140,000 pounds weight of silver and gold over a period of twenty-five years."

"Too right he did, Tan, but just imagine the billions of pounds that sum would be worth today. Well, as it turned out, Sweyn Fork-Beard didn't want any cash; he was after the whole kingdom, which fell into his hands along with the blessing of the Anglo-Saxon Witan, or ruling council, who were by then, to put it mildly, totally brassed off with your friend 'Useless'.

"Sweyn died on 4 February AD 1014 and his son, the nineteen-year-old Knud, failed to gain the support of the Witan, which unexpectedly asked Aethelred to come back to England. All would be forgiven, apparently, provided Aethelred turned over a new leaf, which he promised to do. However, after thirty-five years of total misrule, Aethelred, like the proverbial leopard, couldn't change his spots! He reverted to his usual style of incompetent kingship!"

"I'm utterly convinced there's a point to this story," said Tan, almost at the end of his tether . . . and one which is relevant to both Gosforth and Cumbria."

"Tan, you have the attention span of a gnat with a stroke! Well, in a Cnut-shell, Knud returned in AD 1015 and Aethelred died the following year. Another Edmund, Aethelred's son, came to an agreement with Canute, which probably wasn't that wise as within two months Edmund was found dead, either riddled with crossbow bolts or punctured by numerous stab wounds."

"So Knud, or Canute, became King of England."

"Just so, Tan – he was already the King of Denmark, to which he had added the crowns of Norway and half of Sweden – he truly was a Great Dane."

"So . . . ?"

"Well, Canute, who is really only known for the ridiculous story of his failure to turn back the tide while seated on a throne on an unknown beach, actually played a vital role in the history of Cumbria!"

"Finally!" said Tan.

"In AD 1018 Malcolm II, King of Scotland invaded and captured the northernmost part of Northumbria – the region now known as Lothian. Canute wasn't all that fussed about losing Lothian – rubbish footballers even then – and probably couldn't be bothered to try to take it back. Malcolm was oblivious to this, but when Canute proposed a swap of Northern Cumbria – the part which was the southern tip of Strathclyde – for Lothian he agreed, not wanting to take on the might of the Great Dane."

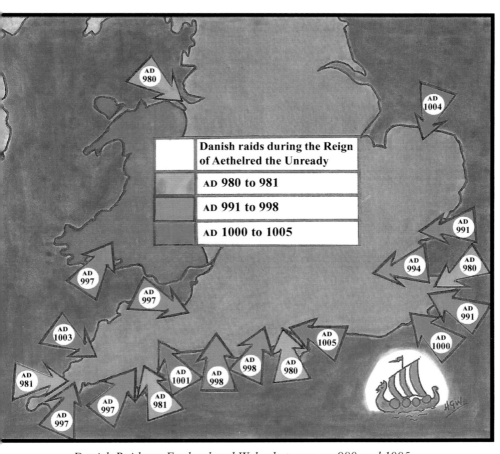

Danish Raids on England and Wales between AD 980 and 1005 – resulting in the extortion of 140,000 pounds of Danegeld from England's King Aethelred the Unready.

Knud – the Great Dane.

"So, that is why the present border between the two countries is as it is now." Tan sighed with relief.

"Yes, and that essentially was the Eighth Scandinavian Invasion of Britain, which ended in AD 1045 with what is now referred to as the Second Restoration of the House of Wessex, when Edward the Confessor, who was the son of Aethelred the Unready and his wife, Emma of Normandy, was crowned King of England."

At that exact moment, they drew up in front of St Mary's Church in Gosforth and were met by the Reverend Gunnar Mangison, whose name, when translated from the Old Norse, means 'Gunnar, the son of no one in particular'.

"Good afternoon, boys," he said with a welcoming smile. "Your fame has preceded you. I have invited you here not to talk about U664, as you might have supposed, but to see our cross, which is quite unusual. It is in fact the tallest Anglo-Norse cross in the country. However, it's not at all like the famous St Martin's Cross on Iona, on which I fear my distant ancestors may have carved their names when they burned down St Columba's monastery.

"Our cross's claim to fame is on account of its carvings. The upper ones are Anglo-Saxon and Christian, whereas those at the bottom depict stories from Norse mythology. It's just over there – be my guest."

With that he turned on his heels and slowly sauntered toward the vicarage.

Tan turned to Yan and, half aghast, said, "He just winked at me!"

"Don't be silly – vicars don't wink! You must have been thinking about Salvador Dali."

"No, I wasn't – I was actually thinking about football referees."

The cross was indeed exactly as described, but on its far side, virtually hidden from view, was another clergyman, kneeling on the grass clipping away with secateurs.

"More tea, vicar?" said Tan.

"Pardon?"

"My brother wondered if you were the Reverend Mangison's curate."

"No, I am the vicar of this parish. And who is this imposter, Mangison?" snapped back the normally even-tempered clergyman, his hand leaning against the cross.

Just at that precise moment a shaft of light hit a carving next to his hand, which was resting on the dull-red grimy lichen-encrusted sandstone cross. The image seemed to glow momentarily, revealing a small richly coloured tableau of a large coiled serpent, a kneeling woman and a bound screaming man whose contorted features were unmistakably those of the Reverend Gunnar Mangison.

"Then who is that?" Yan and Tan demanded to know.

The vicar stood up and, realising he had been a little offhand, apologised.

"That is Loki, one of the so-called gods of Asgard, who was tied to a slab of stone in a cave with the entrails of his own son, Narvi, for causing the death of Balder, the son of Odin and Frig. Loki had encouraged Hod, the blind brother of Balder, to throw a dart made of mistletoe at Balder, which killed him. As part of the punishment, a large poisonous snake was secured to a stalactite above Loki, who had to endure the constant dripping of venom on to his face. The woman is Loki's wife, Sigyn, who is holding a chalice to catch the venom, which she emptied when full, causing once more the poison to fall on to his face and his agonising screams to echo around the cave."

On the journey back home the penny finally dropped with a thud almost as loud as Loki's screams. Both boys simultaneously thought the same thing, but, as ever, Yan was the first to speak.

"So, that's what Fatha meant. It was Loki all the time . . . but how many of the others were also that mischievous shape-changer?"

"What woolly heads we've been – missed every clue, every single one, and all the time he was just dictating to us his history of Cumbria . . . but, Yan, do you think Loki was also really trying deep down to tell us something else?"

"Yes, I do; but I have to ask, have you by any chance . . . on your person . . . a banana?"

"No, but I did notice the grass on the fells looks particularly tasty this time of year, Yan!"

* * * * *

As for those of you who may be doubting the scientific validity of this Cumbrian yarn, I have to tell you that evolution, most assuredly, does **not** run in a straight line . . . but as for the rest, well, you'll have to make your own minds up.

Oh, yes, and while we're at it, when next you find yourself driving along the backroads to Mungrisdale and happen to spot a couple of curious Herdwick sheep by the side of the road . . . smiling at you . . . please say hello to Yan and Tan for me.

Professor Tethra Hardwick.

Gosforth Cross – St Mary's Church: 'Loki and Sigyn'.

THE APPENDICES

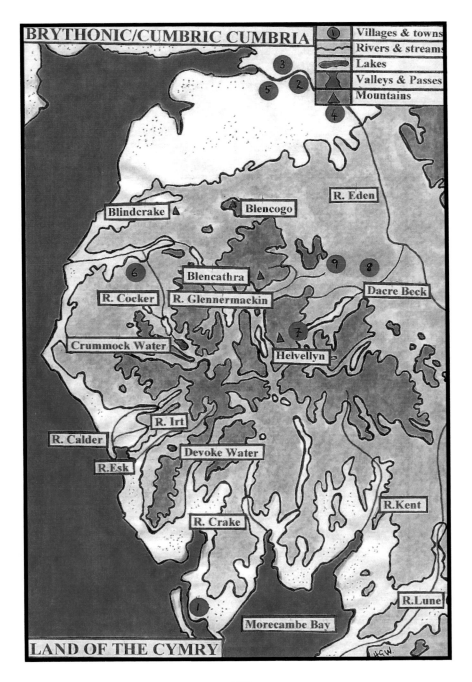

BRYTHONIC/CUMBRIC CUMBRIA

	Villages & towns
	Rivers & streams
	Lakes
	Valleys & Passes
	Mountains

Blindcrake

Blencogo

R. Eden

R. Cocker

Blencathra

R. Glennermackin

Dacre Beck

Crummock Water

Helvellyn

R. Irt

R. Calder

Devoke Water

R.Esk

R.Kent

R. Crake

R.Lune

Morecambe Bay

LAND OF THE CYMRY

H.C.W.

138

BRYTHONIC/CUMBRIC CELTIC NAMES

Areas
1. Cumbria = land of the **Cymry** (people).
2. Morecambe Bay = **mori** + **kambo** = crooked sea.

Towns and Villages *(numbered red on map, page 138)*
1. Barrow-in-Furness = **barr** + **ey** (AS) = island next to the headland.
2. Carlisle = **caer** + **leul** (AS) = fort dedicated to the Celtic deity Lugi.
3. Cargo = **craig** = the craggy place.
4. Cumwhitton = **Cymry** + **ton** (AS) = village of the **Cymry** (people).
5. Drumburgh = **drum/trum** + **burgh** (AS) = fort on the ridge.
6. Eaglesfield = **Eccles** + **feld** (AS) = open land/field near the church.
7. Glenridding = **glinn** + **rhedyn** = valley with ferns and bracken.
8. Penrith = **penn** + **rid** = hill by the ford.
9. Penruddock = **penn** + **rhudd** = red hill.

Rivers
1. Calder = **kaleto** = rocky and fast-flowing (river).
2. Cocker = **kukra** = crooked or winding (river).
3. Crake = **kraki** = stony (river).
4. Dacre Beck = **dakru** + **brekkr** (N) = trickling stream.
5. Eden = known as **ituna** = river with the rushing water.
6. Esk = **isca** = water.
7. Glenermackin = **glyndwfr** + **mochyn** = river valley of the pig.
8. Irt – **ir** = a river with fresh water.
10. Kent = **cunetio** = sacred (river).
11. Lune = **alona** = pure or healthy river.

Lakes
1. Crummock Water = **crumbaco** = lake with the crooked river.
2. Devoke Water = **dubaco** = small dark tarn.

Mountains and Hills
1. Blencathra = **blen** + **cadeir/cuthol** = the summit of the seat-like mountain (saddleback) or Devil's Peak.
2. Blencogo = **blen** + **cogo** = summit where the cuckoos can be found.
3. Blindcrake = **blenn** + **craig** = hill with the rocky summit.
4. Helvellyn = **hal** + **velyn** = hill topped with yellow moorland.

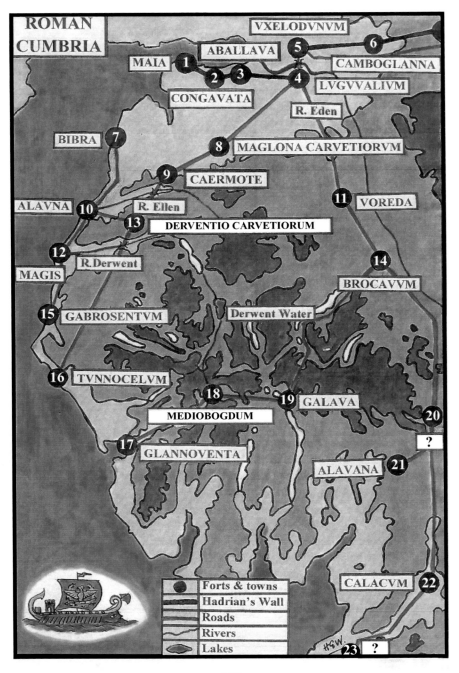

ROMAN CUMBRIA

VXELODVNVM

MAIA **1**

ABALLAVA

5

6

CAMBOGLANNA

2 **3**

4

CONGAVATA

LVGVVALIVM

R. Eden

BIBRA **7**

8 MAGLONA CARVETIORVM

9 CAERMOTE

ALAVNA **10**

R. Ellen

11 VOREDA

13 DERVENTIO CARVETIORUM

12

R. Derwent

14

MAGIS

BROCAVVM

15 GABROSENTVM

Derwent Water

16 TVNNOCELVM

18

19 GALAVA

MEDIOBOGDUM

20

17 GLANNOVENTA

?

ALAVANA **21**

CALACVM **22**

●	Forts & towns
▤	Hadrian's Wall
	Roads
	Rivers
	Lakes

23 ?

140

THE ROMANS IN CUMBRIA
(Key to Map on Page 140)

The Wall Forts (from West to East)

1. Bowness-on-Solway – **Maia** – the fort dedicated to the mother of Mercury by Jupiter, but this fort, the most westward fort, was known as 'The Larger Fort'.
2. Drumburgh – **Congavata**.
3. Burgh by Sands – **Aballava** – orchard.
4. Carlisle – **Luguvalium** – the city dedicated to Lugus (a deity in the Celtic pantheon).
5. Stanwix – **Uxelodunum** or **Petriana** – waterside fort – a large cavalry fort on the north bank of the Eden (or Itouna) opposite Luguvalium.
6. Castlesteads – **Camboglanna** – fort near the winding valley.

Other Outpost Forts (from West to East)

7. Beckfoot – **Bibra**.
8. Old Carlisle – **Maglona (Carvetiorum)**.
9. Caermote – **Caermote** – a Roman auxiliary fort.
10. Maryport – **Alauna** – beautiful place (of the Carvetii) – from which the River Ellen derives its name.
11. Old Penrith – **Voreda** – possibly related to **veredus**, a courier's horse or waystation, which in turn may be related to the Celtic word **gorwydd**, a horse.
12. Burrow Walls – **Magis** – ?
13. Papcastle – **Derventio (Carvetiorum)** – a *vicus*, or civilian settlement, from which the River Derwent and Derwent Water derive their names.
14. Brougham – **Brocavum** – ?
15. Moresby – **Gabrosentum** – ?
16. Beckermet – **Tunnocelum** or **Iuliocenon** – site of suspected fort and port.

17. Ravenglass – **Glannoventa** – market on the shore.
18. Hardknott – **Mediobogdum** – ?
19. Ambleside – **Galava** – ?
20. Low Borrow Bridge – ?
21. Watercook – **Alavana** – ?
22. Burrow-in-Lonsdale – **Calacum** – flower basket.
23. Lancaster – name unknown.

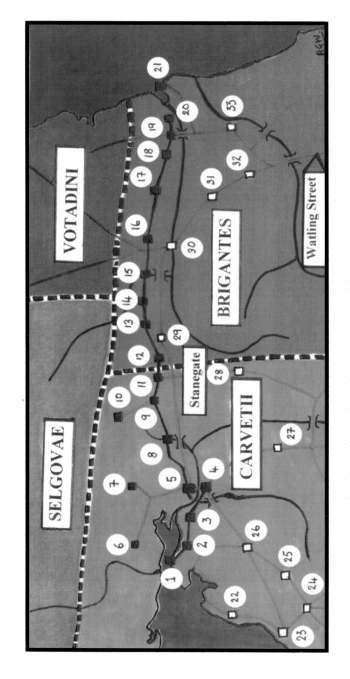

Hadrian's Wall and the Celtic tribes either side of it – circa AD 150.

HADRIAN'S WALL
(Key to Map on Page 144)

The Wall Forts (from West to East)

1. Bowness-on-Solway – **Maia** – the name of the mother of Mercury by Jupiter.
2. Drumburgh – **Congavata** – place.
3. Burgh-by-Sands – **Aballava** – orchard.
4. Carlisle – **Luguvalium** – city of the strength of Lugus (a deity in the Celtic pantheon).
5. Stanwix – **Uxelodunum** or **Petriana** – latinised form of a Celtic place name.
6. Birrens – **Blatobulgium**.
7. Netherby – **Castra Exploratum** – secure fortress.
8. Castlesteads – **Camboglanna** – bent valley.
9. Birdoswald – **Banna** – ?
10. Bewcastle – **Fanum Cocida** – shrine of Cocidius (a northern British Celtic deity).
11. Carvoran – **Magnis** or **Magnae Caretiorum** – greats of the Carvetii.
12. Great Chesters – **Aesica** – ?
13. Housesteads – **Vercovicium** or **Borovicium** – village (*vicus*) on the slope.
14. Carrawburgh – **Brocolitia** – latinised version of a Celtic place name meaning badger holes.
15. Chesters – **Cilurnum** – ?
16. Haltonchesters – **Onnum** – ?
17. Rudchester – **Vindobala** – white strength.
18. Benwell – **Condercum** – ?
19. Newcastle – **Pons Aelius** – the Aelian Bridge (Hadrian's family clan name was Aelius).
20. Wallsend – **Segedunum** – place of strength.
21. South Shields – **Arbeia** – fort of the Arab Troops (it was once garrisoned by Mesopotamian Boatmen).

The Outpost Forts (from West to East)

22. Beckfoot – **Bibra** – ?
23. Maryport – **Alauna** – related to the local River Ellen.
24. Papcastle – **Derventio** – seems to be related to the Latin name for the River Cocker.
25. Caermote – ?
26. Old Carlisle – **Olenacum** – ?
27. Old Penrith – **Voreda** – ?
28. Whitley Castle – **Epiacum** – the Property of Eppius (a local Celtic tribal leader).
29. Vindolanda – **Vindolanda** – ?
30. Corbridge – **Corstopium/Coriosopitum** or **Coria** – Celtic name for tribal centre.
31. Ebchester – **Vindomora** – edge of the black moor.
32. Lanchester – **Longovicium** – latinised version of two Brythonic Celtic names meaning ship and warrior.
33. Chester-le-Street – **Concangis** – Brythonic Celtic word meaning horse people.

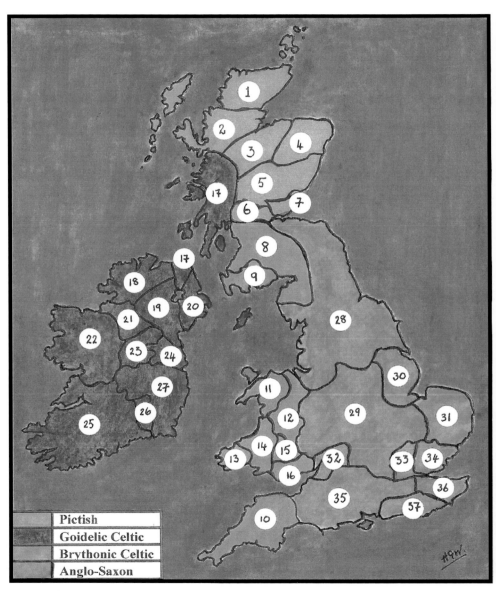

Anglo-Saxon Britain – circa AD 700 – and the different languages spoken across the kingdoms.

THE KINGDOMS OF BRITAIN – CIRCA AD 700
(Key to Map on Page 148)

The Pictish Kingdoms
1. Cait or Cat – modern Caithness and Sutherland.
2. Fidach – the land around modern Inverness.
3. Fortrui – modern Moray.
4. Ce – modern Mar and Buchan.
5. Circinn or Circind – modern Angus and Means.
6. Fotla – modern Athol.
7. Fib – modern Fife.

The Brythonic-Speaking Celtic Kingdoms of Mainland Britain
8. Alt Clut/Clud or Strathclyde.
9. Galwyddel – modern Galloway.
10. Dumnonia – modern Cornwall, Devon and part of Somerset.

The Brythonic-Speaking Celtic Kingdoms in Cymry/Wales
11. Gwynedd – most of modern North-West Wales and Anglesey.
12. Powys – East and Mid Wales.
13. Seisyllwg – modern coastal West and South Wales).
14. Dyfed – modern Cardiganshire, Carmarthenshire and Pembrokeshire.
15. Brycheinog – modern Breconshire.
16. Gwent – coastal South-East Wales.

The Goidelic-Speaking Kingdoms of Mainland Britain
17. Dal Riata – modern coastal Western Scotland and North-East Ireland.

The Goidelic-Speaking Kingdoms of Ireland
18. Ailech.
19. Airgailla.
20. Ulaid.
21. Bryifna.

22. Connachta.
23. Mide.
24. Brega.
25. Mumu.
26. Osraige.
27. Laigin.

The Anglo-Saxon Kingdoms of Britain
28. Nordanhymbra or Northumbria.
29. Mercna or Mercia.
30. Lindisware – modern Lincolnshire.
31. East Engle – modern East Anglia.
32. Hwicce – parts of modern Worcestershire, Warwickshire and Gloucestershire.
33. Middel Seaxe – modern Middlesex.
34. East Seaxe – modern Essex.
35. West Seaxe or Wessex.
36. Cantware – modern Kent.
37. Suth Seaxe – modern Sussex.

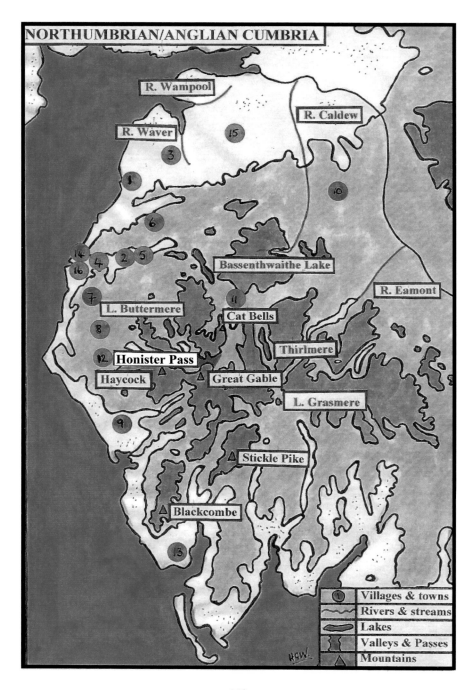

NORTHUMBRIAN/ANGLIAN CUMBRIA

R. Wampool

R. Caldew

R. Waver

3

15

1

10

6

14

4 2 5

16

Bassenthwaithe Lake

R. Eamont

7

L. Buttermere

4

Cat Bells

8

Thirlmere

12 **Honister Pass**

Haycock

Great Gable

L. Grasmere

9

Stickle Pike

Blackcombe

13

	Villages & towns
	Rivers & streams
	Lakes
	Valleys & Passes
△	Mountains

HGW

ANGLO-SAXON NAMES

Areas
1. Cumberland = **Cumbra** + **land** = land of the **Cymry**.
2. Furness = **fuorr** + **nes** (N) = furthermost promontory.
3. Westmorland = **west** + **mor** + **inga** + **land** = western moors of England.

Towns and Villages *(numbered red on map, page 152)*
1. Allonby = **Allon** + **bye** = Allon's/Allen's village.
2. Brigham = **brycg** + **ham** = village near the bridge.
3. Bromfield = **brum** + **feld** = brown or open field, or field where the broom (ME) grows.
4. Camerton = **Cafmaer** + **ton** = Cafmaer's farmstead.
5. Cockermouth = **kukra** + **muda** = crooked river's mouth.
6. Dearham = **doer** + **ham** = village near the deer herds.
7. Distington = **Dyst** + **inga** + **tun** = village of Dyst's sons or people.
8. Frizington = **Fris** + **tun** = settlement of the Friesen people.
9. Gosforth = **gos** + **ford** = village next to the goose track or ford.
10. Inglewood = **Engla** + **wudu** = wood of the Angles.
11. Keswick = **caes** + **wik** = cheese farm.
12. Meadley = **maed** + **leah** = meadow in the woodland clearing.
13. Millom = **millen** = place with the mills.
14. Seaton = **sae** + **tun** = the village by the sea.
15. Wigton = **Wicgr** + **tun** = Wicgr's village.
16. Workington = **Weorc** + **inga** + **tun** = the settlement/village of Weorc's people/sons.

Rivers
1. Caldew = **cald** + **ea** = stream with the cold river.
2. Eamont = **ea** + **mot** = meeting of the rivers.
4. Wampool = Woden's Pool.
5. Waver = **wave** + **ea** = restless stream.

Lakes

1. Bassenthwaite Lake = **Beaban** + *pveit* (N) = Bastun's thwaite (cleared wild land).
2. Buttermere = **buture** + **mere** = lake surrounded by rich dairy pastures (butter).
3. Grasmere = **graes** + **mere** = lake surrounded by pastures (grass).
4. Thirlmere = **thyrel** + **mere** = lake with the narrow waist.

Mountains and Hills

1. Black Combe = **blaec** + **combe** = dark crested mountain.
2. Cat Bells = **catt** + **belde** (ME) = hill with the wildcat's den.
3. Great Gable = **great** + **gafl** (N) = hill with the wide top.
4. Haycock = **heg** + **cocc** = the hilltop shaped like a heap of hay.
5. Honister Pass = **Huni** or **Hunn** + ? = Huni's or Hunn's ?
6. Stainmore = **stan** + **mor** = the stone-strewn moor.
7. Stickle Pike = **sticel** + **pic** = a steep peak.

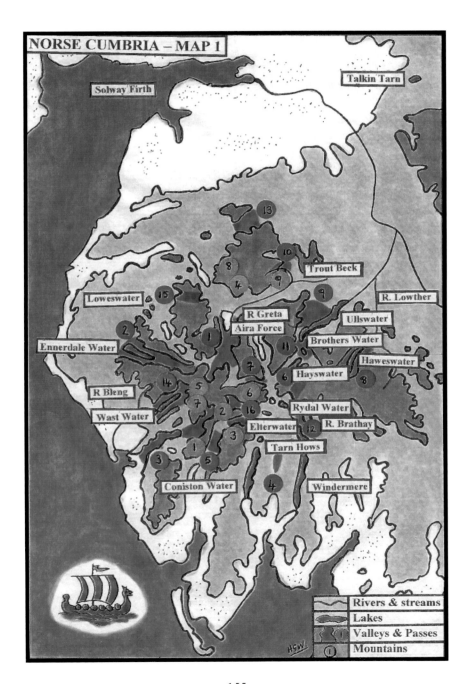

NORSE CUMBRIA – MAP 1

Solway Firth

Talkin Tarn

Trout Beck

Loweswater

R. Lowther

R Greta
Aira Force

Ullswater

Ennerdale Water

Brothers Water

Haweswater

R Bleng

Hayswater

Wast Water

Rydal Water

Elterwater

R. Brathay

Tarn Hows

Coniston Water

Windermere

Rivers & streams
Lakes
Valleys & Passes
Mountains

155

NORSE CUMBRIA – MAP 2

Villages & towns

156

NORSE NAMES

Areas
1. Copeland = **kaupa** + **land** = bought land.
2. Grizedale = **gris** + **dalr** = pig's valley.
3. Solway Firth = **sol** + **vath** + **fjordr** = the muddy narrow inlet.

Towns and Villages *(numbered green on map, page 156)*
1. Aikton = **eik** + **tun** = village by the oak trees.
2. Ambleside = **Amelt** + **saetr** = sheiling or summer pasture at Amelt, which means the sandbank by the river.
3. Appleby = **apaldr** + **by** = village with the apple trees.
4. Applegarth = **apaldr** + **gardr** = apple garth or enclosure of apple trees.
5. Ashness = **eski** + **nes** = the headland where the ash trees grow.
6. Askham = **aski** + **ham** = hamlet with the ash trees.
7. Aspatria = **Patrick** + **asc** = Patrick's ash trees.
8. Bassenthwaite = **Bastun** + **þveit** = Bastun's clearing.
9. Beckfoot = **bekkr** + **fotr** = foot or mouth of the stream.
10. Blennerhasset = **blein** + **haysaetr** = hay farm on the hill.
11. Bootle = **budl** = huts/shelter.
12. Bowness-on-Solway = **bogi** + **nes** = bow-shaped promontory on the Solway.
13. Bowness-on-Windermere = ditto for Windermere.
14. Caldbeck = **kaldr** + **bekkr** = place with the cold beck.
15. Curthwaite = **kirkja** + **þveit or thveit** = church in the clearing.
16. Hawkshead = **haukr** + **heved** = place of the hawk's head.
17. High Hesket = **eski** + ? = ash tree. . . .
18. Low Hesket = ditto.
19. Kendal = **Kent** + **dalr** = valley of the river Kent.
20. Kirkby = **kirk** + **by** = village with a church.
21. Kirkstone = **kirk or kirkja** + **stein** = church stone.
22. Langwathby = **lang** + **wath** + **byr** = village by the long ford.
23. Papcastle = **papi** + **caster** (AS) = (Roman) fort inhabited by a hermit.

24. Portinscale = portcwene (AS) + **skali** = harlot's or townswoman's hut.
25. Seascale = **saer** + **skali** = hut by the sea.
26. Seathwaite = **sef** + *p*veit = clearing surrounded by sedges.
27. Seatoller = **saetr** + **elri** = shieling with Alders.
28. Sebergham = **setberg** + **heima** = abode on the flat-topped hill.
29. Silloth = **sae** (AS) + **barn** = place by the sea with barns.
30. Stonethwaite = **stein** + *p*veit = clearing in the ctones.
31. Threlkeld = *p*rael **(thrael)** + **kelda** = thrall's well (slave's well).
32. Thornthwaite = **hagthorn** + *p*veit = clearing by the hawthorns.
33. Ulpha = **ulfr** + **haugr** = wolf's hill.
34. Ulverston = **Ulfr** + **tun** = Ulfr's farmstead.
35. Whitehaven = **hvit** + **hafn** = white harbour.
36. Watendlath = **vatn** + **endi** + **hlada** = barn at the end of the water.
37. Wray = **vra** = a remote secluded place.

Rivers
1. Aira Force = **a** + **eyrr** + **fors** = waterfall on the gravel-banked stream.
2. Bleng = **blaegir** = dark (river).
3. Brathay = **breidr** + **a** = broad (river).
4. Greta = **grjot** + **a** = rocky (river).
5. Lowther = **laudr** + **a** = foaming (river).
6. Trout Beck = **truth** (AS) + **bekkr** = stream with the brown trout.

Lakes
1. Brothers Water = **breidr** + **vatn** = brother's water.
2. Coniston Water = **konig** + **tun** = the King's farmstead.
3. Elterwater = **elt** + **vatn** = lake with the swans.
4. Ennerdale Water = **Anudar** + **dalr** + **vatn** = the lake in Anund's valley.
5. Haweswater = **hafr** + **vatn** = Hafr's or he-goat's lake.
6. Hayes Water = **Eithr** + **vatn** = Eithr's lake.
7. Loweswater = **laufsaer** + **vatr** = leafy lake surrounded with woods.
8. Rydal Water = **ryge** + **dalr** + **vatr** = lake in the valley where the rye is grown.
9. Talkin Tarn = **tal** (B) + **tjorn** = tarn on the brow of the hill.
10. Tarn Hows = **tjorn** + **haugr** = tarn on the hilltop.

11. Ullswater = **Ulf** + **vatn** = Ulf's lake or **Ullfr** + **vatn** = the God Ullr's lake.
12. Wast Water = **vatn** + **dalr** + **vatn** = the lake in Wasdale.
13. Windermere = **Vinandr** + **vatn** (AS) = Vinandr's lake.

Valleys and Passes – *(numbered dark green on map, page 155)*
1. Borrowdale = **borgar** + **dalr** = valley with a fort; or **bud** + **dalr** = valley with the hut.
2. Ennerdale = **Ehen** + **dalr** = valley with the River Ehen and Ennerdale Water or Annun's dale.
3. Eskdale = **eski** + **dalr** = valley of the ash trees.
4. Grizedale = **gris** + **dalr**) = valley where the young pigs graze.
5. Hardknott Pass = **hardr** + **knutr** = difficult hill climb.
6. Kirkstone Pass = **kirkja** + **stein** = the pass near the stone shaped like a church spire.
7. Langdale = **lang** + **dalr** = long valley.
8. Mardale = **marr** + **dlar** = valley with a lake.
9. Matterdale = **maeddre** + **dalr** = valley where the bedstraw grows.
10. Mungrisdale = **Mungo** + **gris** + **dalr** = valley of St Mungo, where the young pigs graze.
11. Patterdale = **Patrick** + **dalr** = St Patrick's valley.
12. Stockdale = **stakkr** + **dalr** = valley with the haystacks.
13. Uldale = **Ulf** + **dalr** = Ulf's dale.
14. Wasdale = **vatn** + **dalr** = valley of water, or the valley with the lake.
15. Whinlatter Pass = **hvin** + **lettir/leitir** = the pass with gorse on either side.
16. Wrynose Pass = **vrein** + **hests** + **hals** = stallion's pass.

Mountains and Hills – *(numbered light green on map, page 155)*
1. Birker Fell = **bjirk** + **haugr** = the fell with the birch trees.
2. Hardknott = **hardr** + **knutr** = difficult rugged hill.
3. Harter Fell = **hjartar** + **haugr** = deer fell, or the fell where the deer can be found.
4. Latrigg = **latr** + **hryyggr** = sheltered ridge.
5. Lingmell = **lyng** + **mell** (B) = bare hill covered in heather.

6. Lingmoor Fell = **lyng + mor + fjall** = heather-covered moorland fell.
7. Scafell Pike = **skalli + fjall + pik** = peak of the bald mountain, or mountain with pastures.
8. Skiddaw = **skyti/skut + haugr** = the jutting out mountain.
9. Souther Fell = **sutere** (AS) + **fjall** = cobbler's fell.
10. Todrigg = **tod + hryggr** = fox ridge.

BIBLIOGRAPHY

Britain BC by Francis Pryor – Harper Perennial (2003).

The Origins of the British by Stephen Oppenheimer – Robinson, London (2006).

An Invisible History of the Human Race by Christine Kennedy – Penguin Books (2015).

A Brief History of Everyone Who Ever Lived by Adam Rutherford – Weidenfeld & Nicolson (2016).

The Mysterious World of the Human Genome by Frank Ryan – William Collins (2016).

The Ordnance Survey Map of Ancient Britain (1996).

The Ordnance Survey Map of Roman Britain (2001).

The Ordnance Survey Map of Hadrian's Wall (1975).

The Archaeological Map of Hadrian's Wall (2014).

The Ordnance Survey Map: Britain in the Dark Ages (1966).

The Celts, presented by Alice Roberts and Neil Oliver, a two-DVD set produced by IMC Vision (2015).

Roman Carlisle and the Lands of the Solway by Mike McCarthy – Tempus Publishing Ltd (2002).

Romans on the Solway: Essays in Honour of Richard Bellhouse, edited by R. J. A. Wilson and I. D. Caruana (2004).

Romans in the Lake Counties by Tom Garlick – A Dalesman Publication (1972).

The Roman Route across the Northern Lake District: Brougham to Moresby by Martin Allan – University of Lancaster (1994).

Roman Britain by Richard Hobbs and Ralph Jackson – The British Museum Press (2010).

A Short Guide to Hadrian's Wall by T. H. Rowland – Northern History Booklets (1973).

Hadrian's Wall in the Days of the Romans by Ronald Embleton and Frank Graham – Frank Graham (1998).

Hadrian's Wall by David J. Breeze and Brian Dobson – Penguin Books (1987).

The Army of Hadrian's Wall by Brian Dobson and David Breeze – Northern History Booklets (1978).

Hadrian's Wall and the End of Empire by Rob Collins – Routledge (2014).

Birdoswald Roman Fort – A History & Souvenir Guide (1995).

Hardknott Castle Roman Fort by Tom Garlick – Dalesman Books (1982).

Garrison Life in Vindolanda: A Band of Brothers by Anthony Birley – The History Press (2007).

The Antonine Wall by David J. Breeze – John Donald (2015).

Roman Forts in Britain by David Breeze – Shire Archaeology (2002).

Dictionary of Roman Military Terms by Frank Graham – Butler Publishing (2000).

The Armies and Enemies of Imperial Rome by Philip Barker – A War Games Research Group Publication (1975).

A Chronicle of the Republic by Philip Matyazak – Thames & Hudson (2003).

A Chronicle of the Roman Emperors by Chris Scare – Thames & Hudson (1995).

A Companion to Roman Britain by Guy de la Badoyere – Tempus (1999).

Reading Roman Inscriptions by John Rogan – Tempus (2006).

Understanding Roman Inscriptions by Lawrence Keppie – Routledge (2001).

Inscriptions in Britain: Inscriptions on Stone, compiled by Roger Goodburb and Helen Waugh – Alan Sutton (1990).

The Kings and Queens of Anglo-Saxon England by Timothy Venning – Amberley Publishing (2013).

The Anglo-Saxon Chronicle, edited and introduced by Bob Carruthers – Pen and Sword Military (2013).

In Search of the Dark Ages, presented by Michael Wood – A BBC Production (1996).

The Dark Ages: An Age of Light, presented by Waldemar Januzczak – An

IMC Vision Production (2014).

The Penguin Book of Norse Myths: Gods and Myths by Kevin Crossley-Holland – Penguin Books (1982).

Viking Myths and Sagas: Retold from Ancient Norse Texts by Rosalind Kerven – Talking Stone (2015).

Snorri Sturluson: The Prose Edda, translated with an introduction by Jesse L. Byock – Penguin Classics (2005).

The Saga of Ragnar Lodbrok, translated by Ben Waggoner – Troth Publications (2009).

Exploring the World of the Vikings by Richard Hall – Thames & Hudson Ltd (2007).

The Penguin Historical Atlas of the Vikings by John Haywood – Penguin Books (1995).

Blood of the Vikings by Julian Richards – Hodder & Stoughton (2001).

The Northmen's Fury: A History of the Viking World by Philip Parker – Jonathan Cape (2014).

Old Norse Essentials: Grammar, Texts and Dictionary, edited by Volundr Lars Agnarsson (2014).

The Vikings, presented by Professor Kenneth W. Harl – a six-DVD set produced by 'The Great Courses', Chantilly, Virginia, USA (2005).

A Dictionary of Lake District Place-Names by Diana Whaley – The English Place-Name Society (2006).

The Place Names of Cumbria by Joan Lee, Susie Lee and William Rollinson – Kindle.

A Concise Etymological Dictionary of the English Language by the Reverend Walter W. Skeat – Clarendon Press (1901).

Lake District History by W. G. Collingwood – Titus Wilson & Son (1925).